W9-ARI-813

Lilith's Daughters

Women and Religion in Contemporary Fiction

Barbara Hill Rigney

The University of Wisconsin Press

Subjects
1. American fiction- Women authors
   - History and criticism.
2. Women and religion in literature

Published 1982

The University of Wisconsin Press
114 North Murray Street
Madison, Wisconsin 53715

The University of Wisconsin Press, Ltd.
1 Gower Street
London WC1E 6HA, England

First Printing

Printed in the United States of America

For LC CIP information see the colophon
ISBN 0–299–08960–6

For Kim, who weeds the garden

To banish his loneliness, Lilith was first given to Adam as wife. Like him she had been created out of the dust of the ground. But she remained with him only a short time, because she insisted upon enjoying full equality with her husband. She derived her rights from their identical origin. With the help of the ineffable Name, which she pronounced, Lilith flew away from Adam, and vanished in the air.

Louis Ginzberg, The Legends of the Jews, *1909*

CONTENTS

ACKNOWLEDGMENTS

I gratefully acknowledge the encouragement and the assistance of my parents, Juanita and George Hill, and of my friends and colleagues Professors Morris Beja, Lowanne Jones, Mildred Munday, John Muste, Ellin Carter, Richard Bjornson, Lisa Kiser, and Patricia Moots. I also wish to thank the staff of the Ohio State University Women's Studies Library for their assistance in my research.

Lilith's Daughters

INTRODUCTION

What are these ceremonies and why should we take part in them?
Virginia Woolf, Three Guineas

It is not my purpose in this book to reiterate the given: that sexism permeates almost every facet of the major traditional religions, that religious institutions are completely dominated by men, and that ideological reinforcement of this domination has contributed in no small part to the tragedy that has often been women's history. Beginning in the nineteenth century with Elizabeth Cady Stanton's *The Woman's Bible*[1] and Charlotte Perkins Gilman's *His Religion and Hers*[2] and continuing into the present in the works of Mary Daly, Rosemary Radford Reuther, and many others, feminist opposition to the practices and ideas of patriarchal religion has been thoroughly documented. Through literary analysis rather than theological treatise, I wish to explore some of the ways in which contemporary women are perceiving, revising, and exorcising the archetypal images and ideas of traditional religions. My focus here is not an interpretation of what male theologians think about women, but of what women think about themselves and God.

Women writers have perhaps never before been so free to challenge the sacred, to revise and reinterpret the traditional, or to exercise the mythopoetic function in creating

3

new symbols for spiritual transcendence. In *The Second
Sex*, written in 1949, Simone de Beauvoir lamented what
she then saw as the spiritual and literary limitations of
women in her time and before:

> We can count on the fingers of one hand the women who have
> traversed the given in search of its secret dimension. . . . Women
> do not contest the human situation, because they have hardly
> begun to assume it. This explains why their works for the most part
> lack metaphysical resonances and also anger; they do not take the
> world incidentally, they do not ask it questions, they do not expose
> its contradictions: they take it as it is too seriously.[3]

Since the women's movement of the 1960s and 1970s and the
resulting intellectual revolution, a great many women novelists are now asking questions of the world and exploring the
realms of metaphysics to a greater degree than their predecessors ever dared. They are also increasingly aware of the
sexual politics of theology—that many traditional religious
mythologies have been a source of oppression, and that
political freedom is dependent on spiritual freedom. As
contemporary critic Carol P. Christ writes: "Women's
spiritual quest is not an alternative to women's social quest,
but rather is one dimension of the larger quest women have
embarked upon to create a new world."[4]

For some of the writers whose works are discussed in the
following chapters, this emerging consciousness and the
belief that women can be agents in their own philosophical
and political existence manifests itself in a new literature of
protest which is often vehemently iconoclastic. Like
Adrienne Rich, these writers are, first of all, intent on rejecting any belief in a male god:

> Monotheism posits a god whose essential attribute is that he
> (*sic*) is all-*powerful*: he can raze Babylon or Nineveh, bring

plague and fire to Egypt, and part the sea. But his power is most devastatingly that of an *idea* in people's minds, which leads them to obey him out of fear of punishment, and to reject other (often female) deities because they are convinced that in any contest *he* will be victorious. . . . His word is law and the idea of his power becomes more important than any demonstration of it; it becomes internalized as "conscience," "tradition," "the moral law within."[5]

De Beauvoir, too, sees the negative psychological implications of monotheism: traditional religion, she says, is not so much "an instrument of constraint" as it is "an instrument of deception."[6] Throughout *The Second Sex*, de Beauvoir describes what she sees as women's particular need for religion, traditional or otherwise, as a form of weakness, a manifestation of anxiety, a compensation for the loss of power: "There is a justification, a supreme compensation, which society is ever wont to bestow upon woman: that is, religion. There must be a religion for woman as there must be one for the common people, and for exactly the same reasons. When a sex or a class is condemned to immanence, it is necessary to offer it the mirage of some form of transcendence."[7]

The existential atheism of de Beauvoir, however, is not yet a psychological possibility or perhaps even a desirable alternative for most of the writers whose works are the subject of this book. For many, iconoclasm and protest are tempered by the realization that freedom from God and from the traditions surrounding his theoretical existence can be a terrifying freedom. As thinkers like Sartre and Camus discovered, the perception of a universe without God is a recognition of the absolute loneliness of the individual, a loneliness fraught with anxiety, even horror. More than men, contemporary women are confronted with such anxiety in the face of existence. Having rejected traditional patriarchal systems, we find ourselves alone without God and with few conventions or rules to guide us. Psychologist Jean Houston has seen our present state as one of acute and desperate loneliness:

> The age in which we live is shivering amidst the tremors of ontological breakdown. . . . the moral mandates, the structural givens, the standard brand governments, religions, economics, the very consensual reality is breaking down the underlying fabric of life and process by which we organized our reality and thought we knew who and why and where we are. The world by which we understood ourselves, a world which began in its essential mandates two thousand years ago with certain premises about man, God, reality, and the moral and metaphysical order, and which in terms of our existential lives began about 300 years ago with the scientific revolution, is a world that no longer works, whose lease has run out, whose paradigms are eroding, and that no longer provides us with the means and reference points by which we understand ourselves. We are not unlike the cartoon cat who runs off the cliff and keeps on running, treading air over the abyss before he discovers his predicament and says, 'oops!'" . . . There is a lag between the end of an age and the discovery of that end. We are the children of the lag.[8]

There exists an urgency in contemporary fiction in general, but especially in that written by women, to fill spiritual and psychological gaps such as those Houston describes. Some of the writers to be discussed are thus attempting to render the old religious and traditional systems more palatable, screening them in a process Mary Daly would term the "re-mythologizing" of religion[9] to find those ideas and symbols which might prove more politically and philosophically acceptable to women's emerging feminist consciousness. Still others make literary use of such symbols in an ironic way, ultimately finding them necessary only as points of rejection, milestones to be passed on a journey toward self-discovery.

The literary revision of traditional religions begins with a revision of archetypal figures and situations. In the works of a number of contemporary women, the figure of Jesus, for example, becomes not only feminine but a symbol for the female political and social condition. That Christ was persecuted and suffered as a martyr, that he performed the social function of scapegoat and bled for the salvation of humanity, are qualities which lend themselves as literary symbols for the personal and political suffering of women. Certainly, the number of literary transfigurations of Christ has proliferated in recent feminist literature, the images of blood, sacrifice, impalement, and crucifixion becoming more noticeable and identifiable than in the works of earlier women writers. Such victimized and martyred protagonists as Gertie Nevels in Harriette Arnow's *The Dollmaker*, Sula Peace in Toni Morrison's *Sula*, or even the nameless narrator in Margaret Atwood's *Surfacing*, are not merely embued with vaguely Christlike qualities as was the case with such nineteenth-century heroines as George Eliot's Maggie Tulliver or Dorothea Brooke, but are, whether in their own minds or in the minds of their authors, clearly defined and self-conscious Christ figures.

When the author chooses to treat such a literary transfiguration in an ironic mode, as is the case in *Surfacing*, for example, the Christ role and the martyrdom it implies are transcended, and the protagonist is restored to human status. But in those novels in which the author does not treat the female identification with Christ as ironic or as a self-destructive fixation, the stereotypical image of woman as martyr and victim is reinforced; the image of the tree becomes that of the cross.

Much less attractive as a political symbol to contemporary novelists is the archetype of Mary. Most feminist theologians and novelists, including the professed Catholic writer Mary Gordon, unequivocally reject the suitability of Mary as a feminist image, correctly interpreting her role as a composite of patriarchal prescriptions for women. In her humility and submission, Mary is seen as giving birth to Christ but not to herself. Thus, she constitutes yet another Christian symbol which must be examined and ultimately rejected as limiting the human potential of women.

In spite of such negative associations, some writers continue to search for a mother surrogate equivalent to Mary. Perhaps it is another manifestation of modern woman's recognition of her loneliness in the universe that she attempts, through literature, to resurrect ancient goddesses, to construct matriarchal lineages, to filter history in search of mother figures. Mary Daly proclaims the ascendency of the goddess; Elizabeth Gould Davis theorizes the historical existence of lost Amazons and lost continents ruled by women;[10] Harriette Arnow novelistically presents a fallen Demeter. With a somewhat greater degree of ironic consciousness, Toni Morrison depicts black matriarchies in all their mythic dimensions, and Margaret Atwood examines the identification of woman and nature and of pre-Christian religion and female power.

More pervasive in the works of contemporary women novelists and more complex as a symbol for political and religious expression is the archetype of the garden. In some instances, novelists have evicted Adam from Eden and chosen to see nature itself as an essentially female entity, wild and primitive, representing a flight from technology and a withdrawal from society. Thus, Sally Miller Gearhart, in her futuristic novel *The Wanderground*, sees the forests and hills as the only possible retreat for women victimized and brutalized by a male-dominated society. The garden, in this instance, is represented by a totally benevolent and female nature which reflects the innocence of the women who there seek refuge and escape. No fall can occur in Gearhart's garden; even the snakes are mere objects for female curiosity.

Confrontation rather than escape is the function of the very real wilderness garden in Annie Dillard's *Pilgrim at Tinker Creek*. Nature, in Dillard's terms, is violent rather than benevolent and reflects not innocence, but the fallen aspect of the world. It is the place where one discovers God in all his ambiguous beauty and cruelty. On the other hand, revelation of the self rather than of God is the metaphoric purpose of the garden in Atwood's *Surfacing*. Here the protagonist's pilgrimage into the Canadian backwoods is symbolic of her exploration of her own subconscious mind. Here she discovers, not innocence as Gearhart does, not victimization and violence as Dillard does, but complicity and her own human condition.

Another aspect of nature, the ordered and cultivated garden as opposed to the primitive jungle, becomes the focus of a number of other contemporary writers, including Marge Piercy in *Woman on the Edge of Time*, Joan Barfoot in *Abra*, and Margaret Laurence in *The Diviners*. In these novels, the garden is a metaphor for art, for literature itself, and is an expression of both power and beauty.

Whatever image nature holds for these women writers, whether primitive wilderness or ordered garden, there remains a nostalgia for a lost Eden, the sense that, given another chance, we could do it differently. Thus, the figure of Eve takes on a new and powerful significance in such novels as Margaret Drabble's *The Realms of Gold*. Perhaps the contemporary Eve is ultimately the most positive of all the novelistic revisions of Christian archetypes. In recent incarnations, she is not the submissive wife of Adam, nor the temptress responsible for bringing sin and death into the world. Instead, she represents the existential woman who, in full knowledge of good and evil, confronts both the world and her own freedom. Her progress from innocence to knowledge, from a world of myth into a world of reality, is in one sense the archetypal journey implicit in the contemporary feminist novel.

Mary Daly says that the fall of women began in the original garden, not when Eve ate the apple, but when God gave Adam rather than Eve the power to name the world's inhabitants. "To exist humanly," Daly writes, "is to name the self, the world and God."[11] Many of the novels discussed in the following chapters themselves represent a kind of garden wrested from the wilderness of patriarchal language and ideology, expressive of woman's power rather than of her innocence, of woman's passage through mythology and religion toward a confrontation with existence, responsibility, and freedom. They are both exorcism and celebration. They reclaim women's right to name, if not God, then more importantly the world and the self.

1
CHRIST

The tree becomes the torture cross of the world.
Helen Diner, Mothers and Amazons

Because Christ was a man, his fictional counterparts have also traditionally been male, providing a central motif in patriarchal literature for centuries. Even contemporary male authors, nontraditional in many other ways, have focused on a traditionally masculine view of Christ as heroic reformer or at least as active agent in the melioration of the human condition. Theodore Ziolkowski, in his important *Fictional Transfigurations of Jesus*,[1] explores a variety of modern and historical literary Christ figures—none of them female or representative of a female psychology.

The female Christ-figure as a fictional device, whether explicit or only implied, is relatively recent in the works of women writers. While contemporary women novelists are now presenting a great many such transfigurations, these differ from traditional renditions in a number of ways. First, women writers are more conscious of an inherent irony in the depiction of Christ as a woman, and their works are often more pleasurably iconoclastic because of this awareness. Many feminist writers are also more fully cognizant of the

11

political and psychological ramifications involved in the literary transfiguration of Christ; they recognize that women who are oppressed because of their sex often tend to identify themselves with those aspects of Christ which are traditionally associated with the feminine: the essential victim, the eternal sufferer, the innocent scapegoat sacrificed for the sins of an entire world.

Simone de Beauvoir saw such an identification, whether in literature or in life, as a form of paranoid delusion. In *The Second Sex*, she explores women's perceptions of their blood-tie with Christ. As women bleed each month and in childbirth, so Christ bled on the cross; as women perceive themselves as sacrificial victims of men, impaled in the sexual act, so Christ was pierced by the spear:

In the humiliation of God (at the crucifixion) she sees with wonder the dethronement of Man; inert, passive, covered with wounds, the Crucified is the reversed image of the white, blood-stained martyr exposed to wild beasts, to daggers, to males, with whom the little girl has so often identified herself; she is overwhelmed to see that Man, Man-God, has assumed her role. She it is who is hanging on the Tree, promised the splendor of the Resurrection. It is she: she proves it; her forehead bleeds under the crown of thorns.[2]

Phyllis Chesler states in *Women and Madness* that a common manifestation of female insanity is an identification with Christ, an identification "concretely rooted in female biology." According to Chesler, it is through the "blood sacrifice" of childbearing that women assume their role as martyr: "Women are impaled on the cross of self-sacrifice. Unlike men, they are categorically denied the experience of cultural supremacy, humanity and renewal based on their sexual identity—and on the blood sacrifice, in some way, of a member of the opposite sex. In different ways, some women are driven mad by this fact."[3]

A number of contemporary women writers have found their inspiration in the association of woman with Christ, the tree with the cross, blood with glory. The poetry of Sylvia Plath comes immediately to mind and has been frequently and thoroughly explored in this context.[4] A similar preoccupation with woman as victim, in this instance the blood sacrifice equally as complete as Plath's and more terrifying, occurs in Kate Millett's *The Basement*, a harrowing analysis of the actual murder by torture of sixteen-year-old Sylvia Likens in Indianapolis in 1965. Millett sees Sylvia's death, "this head with its frayed lips, this *Pieta*," as a paradigm for the female condition: "You have been with me ever since, an incubus, a nightmare, my own nightmare, the nightmare of adolescence, of growing up a female child, of becoming a woman in a world set against us, a world we have lost and where we are everywhere reminded of our defeat. What you endured all emblematic of that" (*The Basement*, p. 11).[5] To minimize the suffering of Sylvia Likens would amount to a perversity approximating that of her torturers; to see her as a female Christ and her fate as symbolically that of all women, however, is to internalize the psychology of the victim and to deny the reality of female power.

The transfiguration of woman into martyred Christ occurs also in Harriette Arnow's *The Dollmaker*, a novel of immense emotional impact but almost totally lacking in what Ziolkowski calls "the ironic consciousness."[6] Without the detachment that might have been provided by either irony or psychology, Arnow reproduces the suffering and the sacrificial function of Christ in the person of Gertie Nevels, an immigrant from the hills of Kentucky displaced to Detroit during World War II. Gertie herself does not know she is Christ; rather, the transfiguration is imposed by Arnow from without.

The tree, in Arnow's novel, quite literally becomes the

cross. Gertie is a wood carver, a sculptor of great natural talent. Throughout the novel, she carries with her, on both her physical and spiritual journeys, an immense block of cherry wood, itself a kind of cross, from which she plans to carve the face of Christ. She is never to complete the project, however, because a model is never recognizable, even when she looks into a mirror or at the faces of her friends, women who also suffer and are Christ.

In the beginning of the novel, when Gertie is at home in the relative paradise of Kentucky, working the land, loving her children, talking to the trees, and at one with nature and herself, she envisions the potential face of her Christ as "a laughing Christ uncrowned with thorns and with the scars of the nail holes in his hands all healed away; a Christ who had loved people, had liked to mingle with them and laugh and sing" (*The Dollmaker*, p. 64). Like Gertie herself, this Christ is a carpenter, a working person intent on the joy of work; the image is that of Jesus at the wedding of the Cana of Galilee.

Unfortunately, Gertie too has gone to a wedding—her own—and her real cross is a patriarchal and religiously condoned concept of marriage. Gertie's mother, always a voice for patriarchal religion, hysterically admonishes Gertie: " 'Leave all else and cleave to thy husband.' She's never read to them the words writ by Paul, 'Wives, be in subjection unto your husbands, as to the Lord' " (p. 141). Gertie complies, packs up her five children, and follows her husband to Detroit, thus beginning a journey through the underworld: "the whirling snow, the piles of coal, the waiting cars, the dark tanks moving, all seemed to glow with a faint reddish light. The redness trembled like a flame, as if somewhere far away a piece of hell had come up from underground" (p. 168). For Gertie, Detroit is "a world not meant for people" (p. 168); her breath on the frozen car window "was at times a reddish pink, as if bits of blood had frozen with the frost" (p.

169). The blood is, of course, symbolically Gertie's own and literally that of her daughter, who is later run over by a train and killed.

In Detroit, Gertie can no longer conjure up her earlier visions of a loving Christ, and the aspect of her cherry-wood carving changes correspondingly. Her Christ is now an image of the crucifixion, an image which reflects the nature of her world, one determined by poverty, by noise and filth and lovelessness and a malevolent God. In her suffering, Gertie herself psychologically resembles this alternative vision of Jesus, "the head drawn back in agony, the thorns, the nails, each with a drop of crimson below it, a great splash of scarlet for the wounded side, the face bearing many wrinkles to indicate agony" (pp. 235–36). Gertie's former pride now reduced to abject humility, she stands to serve food to her seated family in Arnow's version of the Last Supper. Before, Gertie was capable of performing even the miracle of resurrection from death, as she saved her son by performing an emergency tracheotomy with her wood-carving knife; she now cannot even feed her family, let alone muster the power to protect them from death.

Finally, Gertie is reduced to mass-producing crucifixes on her husband's jigsaw and selling them in the street. Thus, she sacrifices her art to necessity, literally and figuratively selling both herself and Jesus. Her still faceless block of cherry wood begins to resemble her own schizoid self, assuming the aspect of Judas as well as Christ. As Joyce Carol Oates has written in an afterword to *The Dollmaker*:

The novel resolves itself in a bitter irony as Gertie betrays herself, giving up her unique art in order to make herself over into a kind of free-lance factory worker, turning out dolls or foxes or Christ, on order; she is determined to be Judas, to betray the Christly figure in the piece of wood she never has enough time to carve out, and the Christly figure is at once her own and that of the millions of people, Americans like herself, who might have been models for Christ. They do not emerge out of the wood, they do not become incarnated in time, they are not given a face or a voice. They remain mute, unborn. Man is both Christ and Judas, the sacred, divine self and the secular, betraying, human self, the self that must sell itself for "future food" because this is the foreordained lot of man (pp. 603–4).

Gertie, at least, is a physical survivor. But, as I have argued with Arnow in an unpublished interview,[7] surely Gertie has, in emulation of Christ, sacrificed herself as well as her sculpture when, at the end of the novel, she takes up an axe and shatters the cherry wood into the splinters with which she will manufacture more crucifixes. Arnow replied, "She doesn't need it anymore." In retrospect, I think Arnow meant that Gertie has finally come to terms with a "real world" in which God, in fact, would demand the sacrifice of his own son as well as of a multitude of nameless women. There is no room for art in Gertie's universe, only for survival. The only possible salvation for Gertie lies in the sisterhood she experiences with the women in her alley, in the human dignity which they help one another to preserve in spite of the overwhelming odds, which include the very nature of God.

Gertie's reward for her suffering is the mystic's vision of God: she ultimately sees in her neighbors' faces the image of Christ and, in her own, a reflection of a tragic human condition. Like Job, Gertie has experienced an insight into what Arnow, in accordance with the Old Testament, apparently sees as the actual and living God. Also like Job, Gertie remains a victim. She has been sacrificed, not so much by her own volition as by Arnow's grim and naturalistic world view.

More problematic and complex is Toni Morrison's authorial

distance in *Sula*. It is clear that Morrison's protagonist, significantly named Sula Peace, is a composite of archetypal scapegoats: Christ, Cain, even Lilith. Yet, Morrison's third-person narrative technique is so detached, so dispassionate, that we know little of Sula's suffering or of her attitude toward her role. Unlike Gertie Nevels, or even little Pecola Breedlove in Morrison's *The Bluest Eye*, who is raped by her father, made pregnant with his child, and finally reduced to vacant idiocy, Sula does not internalize the psychology of the victim although she recognizes the irony of her situation. In this respect, the character of Sula resembles the more traditional literary transfigurations of Christ and is closer to Ziolkowski's various models than are most female Christ figures. Ziolkowski writes that in many third-person narratives,

we accept the transfiguration when it resides in the hero's ironic consciousness. The author does not invite us to suspend our disbelief totally . . . but merely to savor along with the hero the ironic awareness that circumstances have thrust him into a role sharing certain points in common with that of Jesus. The hero knows that he is not Jesus; the author knows that he is not; and so do we, the readers. But we are all sophisticated enough to enter into a three-way conspiracy of irony.[8]

As is the case with both Arnow's protagonist and with Pecola, however, Sula has no choice about the nature of her martyrdom. She does not heroically choose it; rather, it chooses her.

Like Pilate Dead in Morrison's *Song of Solomon*, whose mythological function is attested by the fact that she was born without a navel, Sula is also marked from birth for a special destiny. On her eyelid she has a mark, the actual shape of which is determined by the perceiver but is variously thought to be a snake, a tadpole, or, more likely, "a stemmed rose" (*Sula*, p. 45). In one sense, Cain, a scapegoat like his mother, was a prototype for Christ. Sula's birthmark is a mark of Cain, and like him, she becomes a pariah, driven out from her community, hated and shunned, left alienated and alone. In her very consciousness of her role, however, and because her mark is that of the flower traditionally associated with divinity, Sula is also a martyred Christ. Morrison's epigraph for the novel, taken from Tennessee Williams' *The Rose Tattoo*, makes her symbolism obvious: "Nobody knew my rose of the world but me . . . I had too much glory. They don't want glory like that in nobody's heart." Morrison is also careful to provide actual dates for significant happenings in the novel, not only to provide structure, but to further Sula's comparison with Christ. Sula dies at thirty, an age close enough to that of Christ at the crucifixion to warrant remark.

Ziolkowski explains that typical of fictional Christ-figures is "the quixotic insistence on pursuing one's own goals in opposition to the Establishment."[9] Unlike the other black women in the community of Medallion, Ohio, who live such proscribed lives ("The narrower their lives, the wider their hips" [p. 105]), Sula claims for herself a rebellious freedom: "I don't want to make somebody else. I want to make myself" (p. 80). In sexual relationships, of which she partakes freely and according to whim, Sula echoes the sentiments of the Apochryphal Lilith: "There was utmost irony and outrage in lying under someone, in a position of surrender, feeling her own abiding strength and limitless power" (p. 106).

Sula's strength and claims to freedom are largely frustrated, however. She is "an artist with no art form" (p. 105), and thus "she had no center, no speck around which to grow" (p. 103). The "center" which Sula lacks is also a conscience or a superego; she is Morrison's version of the Jungian shadow, that part of the human mind which contains a necessary and indispensable evil, that quadrant of the Holy Trinity without which Father, Son, and Holy Ghost are incomplete. The only act for which Sula feels obvious guilt is her complicity in the drowning death of a small boy. In all other instances, she feels guiltless, unconcerned. She watches passively, "not because she was paralyzed, but because she was interested" (p. 67), while her own mother is accidentally burned alive; she seduces the husband of her only friend; she commits her grandmother to a nursing home and assumes ownership of her house.

But it is not for these acts, most of them unknown to the general community, that Sula is almost universally regarded as evil. Her return to Medallion after a long absence is preceded by a plague of robins, an omen of misfortune; her death is folowed by another freak of nature, a catastrophic ice storm. Because of her mark, because of her largely self-imposed isolation, because of this sympathetic reaction of nature itself, Sula is recognized as a witch, and as such, she *completes* the community and thus benefits it. The "medallion" or mandala which inspires the name of Morrison's setting must be finished, enclosed. The people of Medallion somehow intuit this fact:

Once the source of their personal misfortune was identified, they had leave to protect and love one another. They began to cherish their husbands and wives, protect their children, repair their homes and in general band together against the evil in their midst. . . . They would no more run Sula out of town than they would kill the robins that brought her back, for in their secret awareness of Him, He was not the God of three faces they sang about. They knew quite well that He had four, and that the fourth explained Sula. (P. 102)

In analyzing the scapegoat syndrome, Daly writes: "Society as we know it has the perverse need to create 'the Other' as object of condemnation so that those who condemn can judge themselves to be good."[10] Although the community returns to its former amorality after Sula's death, the cleansing function of the scapegoat no longer viable, Sula remains for the people "the most magnificent hatred they had ever known" (pp. 148–149).

There is one citizen of Medallion, however, who, through the vision of his madness, recognizes Sula as an object for adoration. Shadrack, the Holy Fool, sees in her a life principle; she is "his woman, his daughter, his friend" (p. 135), although they have exchanged between them only the significant word which denies death, "always." Since his experience in the war (Morrison's equivalent to the Biblical fiery furnace in which the original Shadrack finds his apotheosis), Shadrack has been passionately concerned with death, and so, in an attempt to order death, to make it rational and predictable, he has instituted "Suicide Day": "If one day a year were devoted to it, everybody could get it out of the way and the rest of the year would be safe and free" (p. 12). The community has come to depend on the annual regularity of Shadrack's ceremonial bell-ringing and his ritual invitation to death, although it is not until just after Sula's death that the people respond. Again, a freak of nature influences the community's behavior; a hot spell in January contributes to the mass hysteria with which the people greet Shadrack's bell. Like the Pied Piper leading away the children of Hamlin in revenge for a bad debt, Shadrack leads a vast number of the people of Medallion into an abandoned tunnel, a womb in the earth, where they perish as the tunnel collapses. Shadrack has finally succeeded in ordering death itself and has made good the town's debt to Sula, its lost savior.

He also completes our view of Sula as Christ by providing for her a form of resurrection, what Ziolkowski refers to as a "mystical transferral of mission."[11] As Sula's disciple, Shadrack has also assumed her mythological function as scapegoat; by ridding the town of its unconscious guilt, he has also purified it.

Morrison provides yet another resurrection for Sula when, at the end of the novel, Sula's ghostly presence is felt by her friend, Nel. For years, Nel has failed to appreciate Sula's role as savior, both in the community and in their personal friendship. She has only nursed the grudge that Sula took her husband from her. Now an aging woman, Nel finally recognizes that her relationship with Sula was her most valuable experience. Transcending sex or marriage, their friendship assumes the importance of a sacred sisterhood:

> "Sula?" she whispered, gazing at the tops of trees. "Sula?"
>
> Leaves stirred; mud shifted; there was the smell of over-ripe green things. A soft ball of fur broke and scattered like dandelion spores in the breeze.
>
> "All that time, all that time, I thought I was missing Jude." And the loss pressed down on her chest and came up into her throat. "We was girls together," she said as though explaining something. "O Lord, Sula," she cried, "girl, girl, girlgirlgirl." (P. 149)

Nel's epiphany reflects only what Sula herself has known perhaps from the beginning. Morrison indicates Sula's consciousness of her role early in the novel, at that point at which she and Nel, as young girls, encounter a number of abusive white boys on the way from school:

> Sula squatted down in the dirt road and put everything down on the ground: her lunchpail, her reader, her mittens, her slate. Holding the knife in her right hand, she pulled the slate toward her and pressed her forefinger down hard on its edge. Her aim was determined but inaccurate. She slashed off only the tip of her finger. The four boys stared open-mouthed at the wound and the scrap of flesh, like a button mushroom, curling in the cherry blood that ran into the corners of the slate.

Sula raised her eyes to them. Her voice was quiet. "If I can do that to myself, what you suppose I'll do to you?" (Pp. 46–47)

Morrison represents this incident both as a puberty ritual and a sacrificial self-castration:[12] Sula has declared her autonomy, but she has sacrificed herself in the process. She is heroic, but nonetheless a martyr. Years later on her death-bed, Sula confides to Nel the consciousness of her signifi-cance and the recognition of her sacrifice to the people of Medallion:

Sula raised herself up on her elbows. Her face glistened with the dew of fever. She opened her mouth as though to say something, then fell back on the pillows and sighed. "Oh, they'll love me all right. It will take time, but they'll love me." The sound of her voice was as soft and distant as the look in her eyes. "After all the old women have lain with the teen-agers; when all the young girls have slept with their old drunken uncles; after all the black men fuck all the white ones; when all the white women kiss all the black ones; when all the guards have raped all the jailbirds and after all the whores make love to their grannies; after all the faggots get their mothers' trim; when Lindbergh sleeps with Bessie Smith and Norma Shearer makes it with Stepin Fetchit; after all the dogs have fucked all the cats and every weathervane on every barn flies off the roof to mount the hogs . . . then there'll be a little love left over for me. And I know just what it will feel like." (P. 125)

Even in this apocalyptic vision, Sula is no prophet, no role model for women. Like the imprisoned imbecile child in Ursula LeGuin's "psycho-myth," "The Ones Who Walk Away from Omelas,"[13] on whose miserable presence the community depends for its health and prosperity, Sula is an incarnation of myth, an archetypal scapegoat. Her political significance is not a celebration of the heroism of black women, but an indictment of society's immoral and irre-sponsible need to create scapegoats in the first place, whether

these be black, female, or both. Sula's last words to Nel—
that she will die heroically, that she will go down "like one of
those redwoods" (p. 123)—are thus ironic. Within the context of the Christian myth of the scapegoat, Helen Diner's
image of the tree as torture cross remains a viable and
dangerously predominant image in the female psyche.

Ziolkowski writes that the most successful literary transfigurations of Christ have been those "inspired by a kind of
'hate,' an aesthetic detachment that sharpens psychological
insight, heightens irony, and receives its fullest gratification
from the play with pure form that transcends all meaning."[14]
That contemporary novel which best demonstrates such an
aesthetic detachment, such a degree of irony, is Margaret
Atwood's *Surfacing*.
    Atwood's nameless protagonist is one of the few female
characters in contemporary fiction to survive both physically
and psychologically the identification with Christ. Her survival, in fact, *depends* on her renunciation of such an identification. Here, as in all her works, Atwood insists on the
necessity for confrontation with a real and existential self, the
discovery of which depends on the rejection of a multiplicity
of possible mythological roles, among them that of Jesus as
innocent victim of the world's brutality.
    As both Carol Christ[15] and Francine du Plessix Gray[16]
have pointed out, *Surfacing* is replete with Christian im-
agery. Both as child and adult, the protagonist is fascinated,
even preoccupied, by the concept and implications of
Christ, very probably because the protagonist's father has
prohibited religion in the same way that other parents pro-
hibit sex: "Christianity was something he'd escaped from, he
wished to protect us from its distortions" (*Surfacing*, p. 63).
In spite of her father's teachings, the child is convinced that
"there was a dead man in the sky watching everything I did"
(p. 52). Even the small community church becomes some-

thing "illicit and attractive" (p. 63). Fascination with religion replaces adolescent sexual curiosity: "I learned about religion the way most children then learned about sex" (p. 52). Even as an adult, the protagonist sees a perverse connection between sex and religion, as she overhears her companions making love in the next room, calling repeatedly on Jesus. Sex is "like death" (p. 99), the protagonist thinks to herself, and women are the victims in this form of ritual murder: impaled, crucified, in the sexual act and in the sexual relationship.

The protagonist's father has tried to protect his children from evils other than religion, moving his family to the Canadian backwoods far from infectious knowledge of World War II and Hitler. For the father, a scientist for whom logic explains everything, even Hitler is "not the triumph of evil but the failure of reason" (p. 68). The protagonist sees both her parents as remiss in their failure to communicate the possibility of evil: "They didn't teach us about evil, they didn't understand about it." Living in their "artificial garden," they were "remote as Eskimos or mastodons" (p. 169). The protagonist and her brother, however, devise a system for themselves, dividing the world into polarities of moral distinctions: "There had to be a good kind and a bad kind of everything" (p. 44). Their childhood games, as recalled by the adult protagonist, incorporate evil in every aspect and include the murder of dolls and insects and the virtual reenactment of war. The protagonist remembers:

We killed other people besides Hitler, before my brother went to school and learned about him and the games became war games. Earlier we would play we were animals; our parents were the humans, the enemies who might shoot us or catch us, we would hide from them. But sometimes the animals had power too: one time we were a swarm of bees, we gnawed the fingers, feet and nose off our least favorite doll, ripped her cloth body open and pulled out the stuffing, it was gray and fluffy like the insides of mattresses; then we threw her into the lake. She floated and they found the body and asked us how she got lost, and we lied and said we didn't know. Killing was wrong, we had been told that: only enemies and food could be killed. Of course the doll wasn't hurt, it wasn't alive; though children think everything is alive. (P. 154)

In the first pages of the novel, the protagonist's memories include a game played with her brother in which they wrapped their feet in blankets and pretended "the Germans shot our feet off" (p. 9). For them, Hitler is the very origin of evil, "many-tentacled, ancient and indestructible as the Devil" (p. 153).

As the child insists that the world is divided between good and evil, so she also perceives it as divided between female and male; for her these polarities are related. Her brother is male and evil, she thinks, and therefore she is female and innocent. She liberates the insects her brother has imprisoned and left to die; she pretends the fish she catches "had chosen to die and forgiven me in advance" (p. 74); she counters her brother's drawings of war and torture with her own pictures of blue skies, sunshine, green grass, and Easter bunnies. She becomes, not her brother's accomplice as before, but his victim. "After a while," she reveals, "I no longer fought back because I never won. The only defense was flight, invisibility" (p. 160).

This assumption of a traditional female role of innocent victim is as devastatingly self-destructive for the adult protagonist as it was for the child. She has, for example, allowed her married lover to persuade her to have an abortion, an event so traumatic for her that she has cancelled it from her conscious memory and invented a less terrifying past. Equally as delusive is her conviction, shared by her present companions, that the invaders and spoilers of the pristine innocence of the Canadian wilderness are power-hungry

Americans intent on the victimization of her country. Another delusion is that she sees her friend Anna as the incarnation of female innocence, bullied and sexually abused by a boorish husband. At this point, the protagonist is still dividing the world into victims and oppressors, still drawing pictures (now she is a professional illustrator of fairy tales) which depict pretty princesses forever pursued by evil giants. She does not realize until later that she herself *permitted* her abortion and thus condoned it as surely as she helped her brother murder her doll, that the invading "Americans" are really Canadians like herself and thus she too is somehow their accomplice, and that Anna is no victim except for her own masochistic pleasure.

In her critical book, *Survival*, Atwood discusses the prevailing theme in Canadian literature as a sense of victimization, both personal and political.[17] Only when the victim's complicity is realized and the responsibility accepted, Atwood argues, is survival a possibility. This applies to the national identity of Canada, she writes, as well as to the individual. Thus, Marian in Atwood's *The Edible Woman* can overcome her anorexic antipathy to food only when she realizes that she has allowed men to "eat" or destroy her and that she has been a participant in her own victimization. Joan Foster in *Lady Oracle* can stop her compulsive eating and increasing obesity only when she realizes that the fault lies not with her mother but with herself. The young heroine of *Life Before Man* must relinquish her hold on an innocent prehistoric world of dinosaurs and giant ferns before she can become truly human and capable of existence in a real world. Similarly, the protagonist of *Surfacing* must stop regarding herself, and by extension all women, as either victimized princess or crucified Christ.

The pervasive symbol of victimization in *Surfacing* is the murdered heron, the bird killed as a trophy by "the Americans" and strung up on a tree in crucifixion position.

The protagonist is horrified to see it "hanging in the hot sunlight like something in a butcher's window, desecrated, unredeemed" (p. 154). She ponders its significance and "whether it died willingly, consented, whether Christ died willingly, anything that suffers and dies instead of us is Christ" (p. 164). The bird represents for her not only the violation of nature and of Canada, but the violation of herself and her aborted fetus. The protagonist uses the same words to record the recognition of her complicity in the heron's death and her cooperation in the abortion: "blood on my hands, as though I had been there and watched without saying No or doing anything to stop it" (p. 154); "instead of granting it sanctuary I let them catch it. I could have said No but I didn't; that made me one of them too, a killer" (p. 170). Atwood has further explained the psychology of her protagonist in an interview: "If you define yourself as intrinsically innocent, then you have a lot of problems, because in fact you aren't. And the thing with her is she wishes not to be human. She wishes to be not human, because being human inevitably involves being guilty, and if you define yourself as innocent, you can't accept that."[18] "The trouble some people have being German," says the protagonist, ". . . I have being human" (p. 155).

In order to come to terms with her own humanity, the protagonist must take a circuitous route, perhaps one not so clearly defined as that indicated by Carol P. Christ[19] or by myself in an earlier analysis.[20] She must, of course, outgrow her childhood and recognize its innocence as illusory. She must stop illustrating fairy tales, both literal and figurative. She must reject her view of a world based on moral polarities struggling in perpetual opposition. She must also overcome her dependence on outside agents, including those that are both Christian and pagan.

For a time, the protagonist rejects one set of gods only to substitute another:

I regretted the nickels I'd taken dutifully for the collection plate, I got so little in return: no power remained in their bland oleo-tinted Jesus prints or in the statues of the other ones, rigid and stylized, holy triple name shrunken to swear-words. These gods, here on the shore or in the water, unacknowledged or forgotten, were the only ones who had ever given me anything I needed; and freely. (P. 170)

Christ now obsolete and useless, the protagonist seeks out other powers, the gods of the ancient Indians whose cave paintings her father had so carefully copied before he drowned in the lake. She fantasizes that "the Indians did not own salvation but they had once known where it lived and their signs marked the sacred places, the places where you could learn the truth" (pp. 170–71). It is tempting to see in these passages some liberating rejection of Christianity and a joyful affirmation of a mystical union with the gods of nature, a nature which reflects the female self and is celebrated through the protagonist's ritualized sex act, which theoretically reinstates her lost child and thus absolves her past.

I think, however, that Atwood's sense of irony will not support this interpretation. Her purpose is not to condone the mystical, but to explore the psychological. *Surfacing* fits quite readily into the literary classification which Ziolkowski terms "psychiatric novels," those in which "the author clearly does not believe in the transfiguration: the fiction is credible because the hero himself, in a delusion that is made psychologically plausible, identifies himself with Jesus and actively seeks out his own Passion. It is, so to speak, the hero and not the author who is organizing the action according to the Gospel."[21] Through an incredibly effective manipulation of the first-person narrative technique, Atwood slowly and subtly reveals the psychopathology of her protagonist and leads her through the curative process.

Sanity, in Atwood's terms, involves an existential confrontation with reality, no matter how dangerous or absurd that reality may be. The past cannot be absolved, only recognized and accepted. The Indian cave paintings are not, after all, "pictographs" to salvation, but merely artistic creations which bear a striking resemblance to the protagonist's own childhood drawings, sharing a similar preoccupation with horned figures, sun motifs, and elongated people. Like Joan Foster in *Lady Oracle*, the protagonist of *Surfacing* has been "an escape artist" (*Surfacing*, p. 83) intent on evading a confrontation with an existential self. She is no more a goddess in nature than Joan is an oracle or the Lady of Shalott or Moira Shearer in "The Red Shoes" or the heroine of her own latest gothic novel (all various mythologies which she adopts to fill the void of her identity). To a greater degree than Joan, however, the protagonist of *Surfacing* is ultimately capable of seeing herself in relation to a real world, a world which, although it includes "the pervasive menace" of the Americans and of the exploiters, can now be "dealt with . . . watched and predicted and stopped without being copied" (p. 221).

Most of all, Atwood's protagonist is not Christ, and with the rejection of this mythology comes the rejection of victimization itself: "This above all, to refuse to be a victim. Unless I can do that I can do nothing" (p. 222). Neither is she an earth goddess or the mother of gods: the child she perhaps carries is "no god and perhaps not real, even that is uncertain" (p. 223). Her dead parents, before elevated to deities, have reassumed their human shapes and become memories rather than ghosts: "They are out of reach now, they belong to themselves more than ever" (p. 222). Nature is no longer a spiritual force, the lake and the trees not now representing redemption, but "asking and giving nothing" (p. 224). Atwood concludes:

No gods to help me now, they're questionable once more,

theoretical as Jesus. They've receded, back to the past, inside the skull, it is the same place. They'll never appear to me again, I can't afford it; from now on I'll have to live in the usual way, defining them by their absence; and love by its failures, power by its loss, its renunciation. I regret them; but they give only one kind of truth, one hand. (P. 221)

Truth, Atwood affirms, is to define the world as it exists and to extricate the self from the multitude of possible mythologies. Withdrawal from reality into myth, whether Christian or pagan, is "no longer possible, and the alternative is death" (p. 223)—or at least the death of an authentic human identity.

Perhaps only when no human identity is at stake, when there is no "reality" to confront, when fantasy is the only norm, can the female Christ figure be regarded without irony by either author or reader. Such is the case in Doris Lessing's *The Marriages Between Zones Three, Four, and Five*, the second volume in her series of allegorical novels entitled *Canopus in Argos*.

Al*Ith is not a human woman, nor does Lessing intend her to be. She is the completely beautiful and ethereal being who is queen of Zone Three, a realm so unlike earth, so almost perfect, that comparison is difficult. Both Al*Ith and her world exist outside of time, outside of space, outside of any human experience except that provided in some fairy tales or perhaps in William Blake's prophetic books. (Blake's *The Marriage of Heaven and Hell* may well have inspired Lessing's title.) Literally and figuratively, Al*Ith does not breathe the same air that we do. Only in such a context, Lessing implies, is Christ a viable entity.

The Marriages Between Zones Three, Four, and Five relates to the earlier *Shikasta* in the same series only in that its setting is one of the six concentric "shells" which make up the universe as described in *Shikasta*. Each shell, or zone, represents a level of consciousness or spiritual development, Zone One presumably being so much beyond the comprehension even of the citizens of Zone Three that it is not even mentioned in either novel. We only glimpse Zone Two, when, at the end, Al*Ith is permitted to ascend into its blue atmosphere as a reward for her compliance with the wishes of the mysterious "Providers," those beings who completely determine events in all six spheres. The consciousness of these super beings, then, is the subject for Lessing's next volume, *The Sirian Experiments*.

The Providers have dictated that Al*Ith should sacrifice herself and her idyllic life in Zone Three to marry the barbarian warrior king of Zone Four. Only in this way can she save her world, threatened by stagnation in its very perfection. She can no more resist such an injunction than Beauty of "Beauty and the Beast" could refuse to save her father from the Beast's idea of justice, or than Psyche can refuse marriage to the monster bridegroom whom she later discovers to be Eros himself. It is in this role as savior that Al*Ith, like Beauty, becomes a paradigm for Christ. Madonna Kolbenschlag's description of Beauty applies to Lessing's protagonist as well:

Beauty is one of the few fairy-tale heroines that we think of as having reached maturity before the story begins. She is in command of herself, she lives in harmonious relationship with her inner world as well as with her surroundings, she is happy. . . . When she gives herself up as ransom for her erring father, it is not a compulsive act, a masochistic reflex or the result of her devaluation of herself. She freely modifies her autonomy in the interests of a higher good. . . . She enters willingly into a dark night of the soul, experiencing fright, confusion and frustration. She looks on the face of a fierce God. By confronting and accepting it, she transforms it into her own likeness, until the spell is finally broken, the beloved one is released and revealed, the kingdom renewed.[22]

In Zone Three, relations between the sexes are completely harmonious and lovemaking is graceful and delightful, unmarred by baser passions. When Al*Ith, escorted by soldiers, arrives at the fortress of Ben Ata, she reacts much like Beauty confronting the Beast: she sees him as "gross, with his heavy over-heated flesh, his hot, resentful eyes, his rough sun-bleached hair which reminded her of the fleeces of a much prized breed of sheep" (*Marriages*, p. 33). Sex with Ben Ata is, at first, brutish, violent, and short. Only when Al*Ith begins the process of educating this almost subhuman man does the novel take on an erotic tone and become a love story. Through her love, Al*Ith succeeds in civilizing Ben Ata and, through him, his entire zone.

In the process, however, she herself experiences passion and becomes less ethereal, more human. She can never live at home in her own world again. When her mission to Zone Four is complete, Al*Ith returns to Zone Three, where she has been forgotten by some and condemned by others as now unfit to rule. She lives, then, a pariah among her own people until the Providers permit her to enter into that state of superior consciousness that is Zone Two. Al*Ith's passage into the blue flames and foggy shapes of Zone Two is strongly reminiscent of the conclusion of Lessing's *Memoirs of a Survivor*, in which the children are swallowed in light and apotheosized as they enter some unknown and higher realm of existence. After Al*Ith's ascension, she is regarded as a legend by her people, who before have scorned her. Only the experience of suffering and passion, Lessing indicates, can provide the passage into more refined states of spirituality; this is as true for entire nations as it is for individuals. The Christian parallel, a variation of the concept of the "fortunate fall," might be that only when God becomes humanized in the form of Christ is human salvation a possibility.

Lessing has not ignored these Christian analogies, although her primary focus is one related to Sufi mysticism. Her cosmology is a kind of ladder up which the individual and collective soul may ascend toward a more perfect state. The individual soul is, in fact, one and the same as the collective soul. The narrator of *The Marriages Between Zones Three, Four, and Five*, the Chronicler of Zone Three, tells us: "We are the visible and evident aspects of a whole we all share, that we all go to form" (p. 197). *Shikasta* bears a similar message reflective of the Sufi philosophy:

Every child has the capacity to be everything. A child was a miracle, a wonder! a child held all the history of the human race, that stretched back, back, further than they could imagine. Yes, this one here, little Otilie, she had in the substance of her body and her thoughts everything that had ever happened to every person of mankind. Just as a loaf of bread holds in it all the substance of all the wheat grains that have gone into it, mingled with all the grain of that harvest, and the substance of the field that has grown it, so this child was kneaded together by, and contained, all the harvest of mankind. (*Shikasta*, p. 167)

In Lessing's terms, all humanity is potentially Christlike. In *The Four-Gated City*, Lessing quotes Idries Shah regarding the Sufi contention that

humanity is evolving towards a certain destiny. We are all taking part in that evolution. Organs come into being as a result of a need for specific organs. The human being's organism is producing a new complex of organs in response to such a need. In this age of transcending of time and space, the complex of organs is concerned with the transcending of time and space. What ordinary people regard as sporadic and occasional bursts of telepathic and prophetic power are seen by the Sufi as nothing less than the first stirrings of these same organs. The difference between all evolution up to date and the present need for evolution is that for the past ten thousand years or so we have been given the possibility of a conscious evolution. So essential is this more rarefied evolution that our future depends on it. (*Four-Gated City*, p. 448)

Lessing's message is still the essentially feminist message of her earlier novels: the personal *is* the political. Al*Ith and her Christlike function, according to the Chronicler, are but manifestations "of what we *all* are at different times" (p. 197). Thus, in Lessing's terms, Al*Ith is not human, but she reflects the human female potential for power, love, and a selfhood that transcends self-sacrifice.

The novels discussed in this chapter represent but a few of the female Christ figures in contemporary literature. For many women writers, all women are Christ, whether for good or ill. The image of Christ, so often negatively applied, might prove a more salutory symbol for women if they choose to identify with the aspect of power rather than of martyrdom, as did a student of mine at Ohio State University:

I was born on the banks of the Ohio River. The same river my great-grandfather and his mule walked across in the winters prior to the First World War. I always looked for the river to freeze to that depth so I could walk the same path, but it never froze that deep again. It never did. It hasn't yet, and I'm still waiting. I am still alive. My great-grandfather is not, but I still know the way across the river. And I am waiting for that time again. . . . One of these days I shall escape the fluid of the land and reach the other side on foot. I will walk on the water to get there if it becomes necessary. And it might.[23]

Perhaps the contemporary woman is also the Anti-Christ, which Mary Daly perceives as shaking the foundations of patriarchy: "The women's movement *does* point to, seek, and constitute the primordial, always present and future Antichrist. . . . this may be the surge of consciousness, the spiritual awakening that can bring us beyond Christolatry into a fuller conscious participation in the *living* God."[24] Daly's ideal, somehow reminiscent of Flannery O'Connor's "Church of Christ Without Christ,"[25] perhaps stops short of the truly radical and revolutionary maxim: women must go even further than "beyond God the Father"; they must go beyond mythology itself in order to find the self.

2

MARY

*And Mary said, "Behold the handmaid of the Lord;
be it unto me according to thy word."*
Luke 1:38

For a number of fictional characters, it becomes impossible to transcend the sex barrier, even in mythology. If they cannot approximate Christ himself, they can at least give him birth. Chesler writes that "women in madness wish to give birth to the world (and to themselves) anew."[1] Assumption of the role of Mary, then, becomes a feminine alternative to the identification with Christ, and provides the added benefit of patriarchal approval. Mary's suppliant assent to the sacrifice of her humanity in order to become the mother of God sums up the qualities idealized for women by Christianity: sacrificial love, sexual purity, humility, passivity. Naomi Goldenberg in *The Changing of the Gods* refers to her as "the good girl of Christianity."[2] Mary embodies the eternal feminine, the glorification of an idea of desexed womanhood that is expressly male-defined.

The central paradox in the figure of Mary, however, lies in a basic confusion of purity and eroticism. While a symbol of nonsexual love, Mary yet represents the implicit eroticism in the traditional relationship between God and woman, the exaltation of the flesh through its denial, the essentially sexual dream of Simone de Beauvoir's mystic: "from blood to glory through love."[3]

Although their theological and historical studies of Mary differ markedly in both intent and focus, Mary Daly and Marina Warner share the conviction that the paradox of Mary lies in her concurrent virginity and motherhood, a state impossible to emulate and therefore punitive in its function as a model for women. Daly writes: "No woman can really live 'up' to it. (Consider the impossibility of being both virgin and mother.) It throws all women back into the status of Eve and essentially reinforces the universality of women's low caste status."[4] Warner has stated a similar view, reflected even in the title of her book: in her virgin motherhood, Mary is truly *Alone of All Her Sex*. Warner writes:

> Mary is mother and virgin; since the sixth century, when the marvelous *Akathistos* hymn hailed her as the one creature in whom all opposites are reconciled, her virgin motherhood has been the chief sign of her supernatural nature. . . . Mary establishes the child as the destiny of woman, but escapes the sexual intercourse necessary for all other women to fulfill this destiny. Thus the very purpose of women established by the myth with one hand is slighted with the other. The Catholic religion therefore binds its female followers in particular on a double wheel, to be pulled one way and then the other, like Catherine of Alexandria during her martyrdom.[5]

Warner further agrees with Daly in her conclusion that the paradox of Mary represents a tool of the patriarchal religious order: "The Virgin Mary is not the innate archetype of female nature, the dream incarnate; she is the instrument of a dynamic argument from the Catholic Church about the structure of society, presented as a God-given code."[6]

Not only Catholic women have suffered on the "double wheel" however. A great many Protestant women writers have also reflected the paradox of Mary in their novels and poetry, seeing in her the conflict between flesh and spirit, self-love and self-sacrifice. For example, George Eliot's novelistic preoccupation with determinism compounded by individual moral responsibility led her to sacrifice the personal happiness of all her major heroines to lives (or deaths) of penance, inevitably in connection with men. Similarly, the nineteenth-century transcendentalist Margaret Fuller recorded a lifelong concern with what she regarded as the necessity for women to achieve the ideal of Mary, thus exonerating the sin of Eve: "Through Woman Man was lost," she wrote in *Woman in the Nineteenth Century*, "so through Woman must Man be redeemed."[7]

Such authors have their contemporary Catholic counterpart in the protagonist of Mary Gordon's *Final Payments*, a novel of great religious violence which remains, nevertheless, religious. The Catholic girlhood of Gordon's Isabel Moore is dominated by the Godlike figure of her father: Joe Moore and God "were fellow soldiers. Because he knew what he wanted, he felt entitled to do anything, and was capable of it" (*Final Payments*, p. 41). The entire community recognizes, along with Isabel, that he "had authority" (p. 79). In his role of patriarch, compounded by the fact that he is a single parent, Joe Moore raises his only and much-loved daughter as his handmaiden; he sees in her all the virtues and attributes of Mary. Isabel, however, recognizes the paradox, the difficulties inherent in living up to such a model; and loving her father "with the passion of mind and soul that he reserved for God" (p. 41), she both rebels against his ideal and contrives to approximate it. She later reflects that she must have deliberately set the stage for the summer afternoon when her father returned early from the college where he taught to discover her in bed with his surrogate, his student. He reacts with horror at the sight of his daughter's bare breasts, at the recognition of his own subconscious sin of incest as much as at her now inescapably evident sexuality. From this point on, the novel is concerned with Isabel's reenactment of penance for original sin, that is, sexual consent as well as disobedience. Isabel is Eve, woman trapped by patriarchal religion and her own fear of the fall into freedom. Redemption can only be achieved, she believes, by abdicating that freedom, forgoing her humanity, and assuming the role of Mary.

Both Isabel and her father initially hope that her sexual encounter will leave her pregnant so that they can resume life together, her penance visible, her Christlike son (there is no doubt in her mind or in her father's that the child would be male) presented to the community as the result of "rape or virgin birth" (p. 20). When no pregnancy becomes apparent, the alternative for Joe Moore is to himself become child as well as father, infant Christ as well as God. He suffers a stroke, "the stoppage of his brain" (p. 21). Isabel spends the next eleven years of her youth (a period of time roughly equivalent to that of Jesus' sojourn with Mary) nursing him, bathing him, feeding him, welcoming her security in the Mary-role, virgin daughter yet mother to her own infant father. She sees her life as a "romance of devotion" (p. 7); "certainty was mine, and purity; I was encased in meaning like crystal" (p. 4).

As the daughter of my father I walked in goodness. I was clothed in the white garment of my goodness, visibly a subject of the Kingdom of God. . . .

As the daughter of my father I lived always in sanctuary. Think of the appeal of sanctuary, the pure shelter. . . . I had won myself a place there as the daughter of my father. . . . I had bought sanctuary by giving up youth and freedom, sex and life. How beautiful, the neighbors said, as I wheeled my father around the garden. I was covered in goodness as if with a tougher skin. (pp. 238–39).

At least in retrospect, Isabel is quite conscious of the ramifications of her choice and of the symbolic nature of her
devotion:

I am the daughter of a father who assumed from the moment of my
birth that I would give him my life. Behold the handmaid of the
Lord, said Mary to the angel; be it done unto me according to Thy
word. As a reward for the loss of a normal life, she became the
mother of God. As the daughter of my father, I thought my fate as
inevitable as hers, as forcefully imposed, as impossible to ques-
tion. I could no more refuse my father than Mary could have
refused the angel coming upon her, a finger of light. (Pp. 327–28)

The Freudian significance of such a situation is, of course,
inescapable; Gordon, in fact, pursues a psychoanalytic ap-
proach to the entire novel. More complex than the mani-
festly evident Electra complex is the Freudian conviction,
which Isabel frequently repeats, that there are no "pure
acts," no gifts without selfish compensation, no sacrifice
without personal reward. Isabel believes with Freud that we
subconsciously arrange even the minor occurrences of our
lives; there are no accidents. Freudian causality combined
with the religious belief in original sin is, for Isabel as it
would be for any person, almost a lethal dose of moral
responsibility. Only the most devout penance, she thinks,
can absolve her guilt. Her penance is a lifelong preoccupation, beginning long before her sexual consciousness. Since
childhood she has felt that she must "pay" for her good looks,
her intelligence. Any small pleasure has its price. Even after
the years of ritual placation ending with her father's death,
Isabel continues what amounts to a masochistic self-indulgence; she invents other kinds of penance, some quite terrible, some only gestures. One such gesture occurs in a
phone booth in Grand Central Station: "In the booth next to
me was a woman, asleep. Her legs were completely wrapped

in bandages; she was obese and nearly bald. She gave off an appalling odor, the distillation of all I feared. But I would not move to another booth. I wanted the discipline of enduring that odor. If I were still in the Church I would have called it a penance" (p. 98).

The woman in the phone booth has her counterpart in one of contemporary fiction's most unmitigatedly evil characters. Margaret, the former housekeeper whom Isabel believes she has prevented her father from marrying, is physically as well as morally repellent, although she represents the sacrificial role for women which the Church has condoned for centuries. (The reader is strongly reminded of Virginia Woolf's "battered woman" in *Mrs. Dalloway*, who is a more sympathetic yet nonetheless horrifying vision of a potential future self for young women.) Margaret is also, for Isabel, a surrogate for her father, a new means of penance after his death, another whip with which to flagellate herself:

I would take care of Margaret; I would devote myself to the person I was least capable of loving. I would absorb myself in the suffering of someone I found unattractive. It would be a pure act, like the choice of a martyr's death which, we had been told in school, is the only inviolable guarantee of salvation. If you died for the faith you would be guaranteed salvation. And when Margaret died, I would simply go on to someone else. I would be the person I wanted to be, beyond loss, above reproach. (P. 249)

In the choice of such a martyrdom, Isabel is only slightly less masochistic than the saints whose lives Simone de Beauvoir analyzes in *The Second Sex*, among them Saint Angela of Foligno, who drinks with delight the water in which she had just washed the hands and feet of a leper, or Marie Alacoque, cleaning the vomit of a sick man with her tongue.[8] Such women have surely gone mad in their excessive zeal for martyrdom. Gordon portrays Isabel's motives, too, as excessive, unbalanced.

By serving Margaret, Isabel attempts to recreate the sanctuary lost at her father's death, to invent a convent for herself. If serving Margaret is not sufficient punishment, she will *become* Margaret, even in appearance. She chastises her flesh through excessive eating, creating "soft pockets of abdominal flesh" (p. 273) (perhaps yet another attempt at virginal pregnancy). In imitation of the bald and obese woman in Grand Central Station and of Margaret, Isabel cuts off her beautiful hair, as nuns used to do. She allows Margaret's "beautician" to arrange her hair in a grotesque bubble style. She revels in her ugliness, considering it appropriate punishment for the "disease" of her sex. Such self-loathing on the part of women is quite usual and even understandable, given the gynephobia of patriarchal religion, Mary Daly would argue: "The entire 'culture' of patriarchy continually generates messages of female filth . . . . through theology and pornography."[9] The "filth" of Isabel's body, she feels, is attested to by the menstrual blood seeping between her legs as she drags herself to confession.

For Isabel, this very blood symbolizes both the abjection and, paradoxically, the exaltation of her flesh. De Beauvoir describes the fanaticism of many deeply religious women in regard to their bodies:

They apply themselves actively to self-annihilation by the destruction of their flesh. No doubt asceticism has been practiced by monks and priests, but the mad rage with which woman flouts her flesh assumes special and peculiar forms. We have noted the ambiguity of woman's attitude toward her body: through humiliation and suffering she transforms it into a glory.[10]

Thus, concludes de Beauvoir, various forms of self-annihilation are in reality the manifestation of the most intense kind of subjectivity, the most flagrant kind of narcissism.

This same kind of paradox—defilement and apotheosis, blood and glory, mysticism and eroticism—characterizes Isabel's sexual relationships with men. Like the protagonist of Pauline Reage's depressing and pornographic *Story of O*, Isabel seeks a bizarre salvation through the masochistic annihilation of her will and her flesh. She is, in one sense, acting in accord with her church's doctrine. In *Alone of All Her Sex*, Warner explores the sadomasochistic elements that permeate Catholic literature and thus reflect a part of every young Catholic girl's education:

> In Christian hagiography, the sadomasochistic content of the paens to male and female martyrs is startling, from the early documents like the *Passion of Saints Perpetua and Felicity* into the high Middle Ages. But the particular focus on women's torn and broken flesh reveals the psychological obsession of the religion with sexual sin, and the tortures that pile up one upon the other with pornographic repetitiousness underline the identification of the female with the perils of sexual contact. For, as they defend their virtue, the female martyrs of the Christian calendar are assaulted in any number of ingenious and often sexual ways: in the *Golden Legend*, Agatha's breasts are cut off; Apollonia's teeth are torn out and she is burned to death; Juliana is shattered on a wheel "until the marrow spurted out," then plunged into a lead bath; Euphemia is tormented with all sorts of refinements and then beheaded; Catherine of Alexandria is also broken on a wheel.[11]

First of all, Isabel seeks out men who are very like her father, God surrogates, who will help her to suffer: "Every man I had known was always saying, in one way or another, 'Give me something. There is something of yours I need' " (p. 150). John Ryan, for example, is described in terms similar to those used in reference to Isabel's father; he, too, is "a very powerful man" (p. 92). A good Catholic involved in social work for the aged, he sins on his own time. He initially seduces Isabel and later rapes her. Isabel perversely endures all this, not merely because John Ryan is thoroughly unattractive to her, but also partly because his position as the husband of her best friend adds to her hoard of guilt.

Hugh Slade is only a slight improvement over John Ryan. He, too, is married; he, too, causes her to suffer, although he provides great sensual pleasure. Isabel struggles to please him: she dresses carefully, bathes meticulously, dashes into a public restroom to dab perfume between her legs lest her flesh offend him later when they are in bed together. At one point in their relationship, Hugh is outraged and even abusive at finding a moldy coffee cup hidden in Isabel's apartment. He punishes her by refusing to sleep with her, having associated the filthy cup with Isabel's sexuality. Thus, Hugh, like Isabel's father and like John Ryan, is a source of penance: he has "an Old Testament back, a punishing back. That was it, there was something I must remember: there was in him the desire to punish" (p. 209). And there is in Isabel, Gordon makes clear, that desire to *be* punished. Only when Hugh decides to leave his wife, making Isabel into "an honest woman," does she again flee from what she perceives as a possible happiness, preferring suffering and guilt: "I saw myself as the public culprit, the woman carried naked through the town, head shaved, borne aloft in a parody of the processions in honor of the Virgin" (p. 239). Even as a parody, Isabel strives to maintain her illusion, her role as Mary, her position in the parade of sainted martyrs.

The great temptation in reading Gordon's novel is to regard Isabel as a victim and to see religion—in this case the Catholic church—as responsible for her condition. Certainly, patriarchal religion historically has demanded the female sacrifice, has condoned the abdication of the individual self in favor of the objective representation of an ideal. In

Gordon's terms, however, Isabel, as well as the Church, is guilty of a sin that is more human than religious: she has used religion as a tool to avoid her own freedom. By accepting a religious concept of guilt, Isabel has postponed the inevitable confrontation with *human* responsibility. The Church, her father, Margaret, her lovers, her penance, and her guilt—all have provided sanctuary from her subjective self and the terror of existential freedom. Frightened rather than saddened at losing her father, Isabel reflects: "Life was space, the borders seemed so far away from the vast airy center that there was no help and I remembered my childhood dream of falling out of bed, through the floor, simply falling" (p. 39). Repeatedly in the novel Isabel experiences what Kierkegaard described as the dizziness upon looking into the abyss. She is, she says, "frightened to begin my life" (p. 127). She nostalgically remembers the safety of her childhood identity: "I thought of Sister Scholastica, who always said to the debating team before we went to another school: Remember who you are and what you represent. I no longer knew whom or what I represented. . . . What if you represented nothing but yourself only?" (p. 165).

To represent the self only is Gordon's message to women. She brings Isabel back from near madness in a pit of grovelling self-indulgence, not, surprisingly, through a rejection of religion, but through a reinterpretation of it. Isabel experiences the love and concern of the good Father Mulcahy, the only person in the novel truly capable of the "pure act." In his alcoholic imperfection, the priest is, ironically, the only man Isabel knows who is not a God-surrogate, but an actual human being. In refusing to hear Isabel's agonized confession of sexual guilt, he provides for her an alternative, though still a religious view—that self-love and self-respect are avenues to a salvation that is simultaneously spiritual and psychological. Isabel thus comes to realize that she is not guilty of her father's death, that universal guilt is part of her delusion. She is still quoting Christ but in a very different context: " 'The poor you have always with you. . . .' What Christ was saying, what he meant, was that the pleasures of that hair, that ointment, must be taken" (p. 298). Isabel concludes: "Christ had died, but it was not death I wanted. It was life and the body, which had been given to me for my pleasure, and the love of those whom loving was a pleasure" (pp. 303–4).

Gordon's conclusion, her plans for Isabel, remain somewhat ambiguous. Isabel will return to Hugh after a brief period of rehabilitation during which her hair will grow and her excess weight melt away. Given her former relationship with Hugh, however, this arrangement hardly seems a confrontation with freedom. The reader is equally puzzled by the necessity for Isabel's "final payment," the expiatory gift to Margaret of her entire inheritance of $20,000. Why, one ponders, is this necessary if, in fact, guilt has been replaced by responsibility, sacrifice by freedom, Mary by a new Eve confronting a new world? Perhaps Gordon wishes to emphasize the idea that Isabel must completely purge herself of any remnant of the old life. At any rate, Isabel's freedom is not purely spontaneous, the psychological burdens imposed by mistaken notions of religious idealism not so readily dispelled.

Meanwhile, however, Isabel is in the company of her friends, two women who have stood by her and understood her dilemmas in a way no man—priest, god, lover, or father—could do. They accept her totally—her obscene hairdo, her obesity. The women are an approximation of the sisterhood which Mary Daly predicts will sweep away the cobwebs of patriarchal religion, substituting what she terms the "ontological spiritual revolution" of the feminist movement.[12] Isabel and her friends represent a new and very untraditional trinity:

And our laughter was solid. It stirred the air and hung above us

like rings of bone that shivered in the cold, gradual morning.
. . . It was so simple and so definite. I knew what I would do. How
I loved them for their solidity, for their real and possible exis-
tences, nonetheless a miracle. For they had come the moment I
called them, and they were here beside me in the fragile and
exhilarating chill of the first dawn. (P. 307)

To experience such a "first dawn," such a rebirth into
one's own humanity, Gordon thus affirms, one must deny
the validity of mythological role-prescriptions like that of
Mary. Certainly Gordon argues a similar thesis in her second
novel, *The Company of Women*. The protagonist of this
novel, whose very name, Felicitas, is part of her religious
burden, is, like Isabel, victimized by a series of God-figures,
most notably the complex Father Cyprian. Like Joe Moore
in *Final Payments*, Cyprian is male power incarnate as he
rejects the world for the love of God and as he dominates the
lives of the women who serve him. Felicitas describes her
mother and the other women as "brood hens circling around
the dying cock whose struts they reverenced" (*Company of
Women*, p. 97), hardly realizing that she, too, is dominated.
Gordon has stated in an interview:

One of the things that most interested me in "The Company of
Women" is female powerlessness in relation to male power, the
phenomenon of women who are very powerful with each other
and very powerful in their own lives and powerful in their outside
accomplishments, but who will suddenly buckle to the authority of
a male mentor, whether it's a priest or professor or a lover.
Women with a kind of zeal to abandon the powerfulness of their
lives to a male who claims authority.[13]

Felicitas, like Isabel, constructs her life around acts of con-
trition for her intermittent rebellions against such authority.
She represents the negative implications of Gordon's message: "Romance believed too strongly too early is damaging.

Whether it's the romance of sexual love or the romance of religion or the romance of political purity, it is damaging."[14]

Many feminist theologians, like Rosemary Radford Reuther, would agree with Gordon that the romance of Mary is particularly dangerous for women: "Mariology cannot be a liberating symbol for women as long as it preserves this meaning of 'femininity' that is the complementary underside of masculine domination."[15] Marina Warner, too, sees the myth of Mary as obsolete: "The reality her myth describes is over; the moral code she affirms has been exhausted."[16]

A number of other feminist writers do not agree that Mary is dead, obsolete, a ghost of patriarchal pontification. Instead, they would resurrect her as a barely recognizable remnant of the Great Goddess of prehistory. Writes Mary Daly:

> What if there has been another manifestation of transcendence whose history preceded the advent of Christianity by many thousands of years, which appeared under different names and forms, which survived in a covert way within Christianity and gave its power over the human psyche? And what if this now is beginning to come into its own again, foretelling a future of spiritual expansion beyond the scope of the Christian imagination's ability to envisage?[17]

"The Great Goddess," Daly argues, has been disguised as Mary but is, nevertheless, "the key to salvation from servitude to structures that obstruct human becoming."[18] Elizabeth Gould Davis in *The First Sex* refers to Mary as "the Female Principle, the ancient goddess reborn."[19] For Madonna Kolbenschlag, Mary is the "anti-myth," she who contradicts the fairy-tale heroines. Writes Kolbenschlag: "In a special way she is symbolic of the passage to liberation which is occurring in women today. . . . She is the One who has first given birth to herself, and thus brings forth God among us."[20]

If Mary had borne daughters, perhaps one might feel more powerfully inclined to embrace such views. The eternal dyad of mother and son, Mary and Christ, however, acts to deny the viability of mother-daughter love. As Adrienne Rich has written in *Of Woman Born*, "The loss of the daughter to the mother, the mother to the daughter, is the essential female tragedy. . . . there is no presently enduring recognition of mother-daughter passion and rapture."[21] Rich then suggests an alternative to the mother-son ideal and presents to us, in beautifully poetic terms, the myth of Demeter and Kore, the daughter's rape by Hades and her abduction into the underworld, the grief of Demeter, and her joyful replenishment of the earth when she is reunited with her daughter. The sequential sadness and joy of Demeter on the annual loss and return of Kore forms the basis of a cyclical myth beside which the death and resurrection of Christ seems an almost pallid approximation.

Certainly, the Demeter-Kore myth now permeates the consciousness of contemporary women writers, who see in it a cultural and spiritual archetype for their own female experience. Women novelists, including Harriette Arnow, Margaret Atwood, and Toni Morrison, have based their works on variations of this central theme.

Arnow's Gertie Nevels in *The Dollmaker* has been discussed in a previous chapter as an embodiment of the tragic Christ figure, but her essential tragedy lies in her metamorphosis from Demeter to Christ, from nature goddess to victim of technology, from pagan deity to Christian martyr, from a representative of matriarchy to a refugee from patriarchy. The isolated hill region of Kentucky, as depicted in the early parts of the novel, has become a matriarchal society; World War II has claimed the male members of the community, leaving the women to farm their lands and survive on their own. Gertie, with her strong arms and amazon height (she stands well over six feet tall), has no problem with this arrangement; Arnow lovingly depicts her chopping wood, digging potatoes, joyful in gathering even a meager harvest. At home in Kentucky, Gertie clearly represents a creative principle as she forces the land to yield, carves tools and dolls from sticks of wood, bears and protects her five children. She has even, as was discussed in the previous chapter, resurrected one of her sons from death by heroically performing a tracheotomy. She celebrates her power, secure in the idea that "she might live and be beholden to no man" (*Dollmaker*, p. 139).

Gertie, at this point, is totally pagan, oblivious to her mother's threats of damnation and the rantings of the lay preacher, Battle John. She walks the land "with long swift strides," singing "at the top of her lungs, joyfully, as if it had been some sinful dance tune, 'How firm a foundation ye saints of the Lord.' She slackened her pace, but couldn't stop the song as she smiled at the stars through the pines. Her foundation was not God but what God had promised Moses—land" (pp. 127–28).

Behind Gertie walks her little daughter, Cassie, "her hair the color of cornsilk" (p. 43). It is Cassie for whom Gertie yearns, more than for her other children, for Cassie is the wild, pagan part of herself, undisciplined inventor of fantasy and of the imaginary witch-child, Callie Lou. When Cassie looks into her mother's eyes, she sees herself reflected: "little bitty girls . . . little Cassies" (p. 54).

The loss of Cassie is inevitable, given the analogy with Demeter and Kore. When Gertie weakens, succumbs to the patriarchal admonition that women must follow their husbands, and joins Clovis in Detroit, she has already entered the underworld. She has forfeited her power and can no longer protect her child. In Arnow's novel, Hades in his chariot come to rape and abduct is death in the form of technology, the phallic and powerful locomotive come to take Cassie into the darkness. Gertie's grief is like Demeter's—inconsolable, profound. Nature, too, reacts, even the April grass becoming merely "green paper" (p. 419), artificial, infertile. But, unlike Demeter whose power remains intact and enables her to seek out her daughter and regain her for at least the larger part of every year, Gertie only grieves. Adrienne Rich writes of Demeter and Kore: "Each daughter, even in the millennia before Christ, must have longed for a mother whose love for her and whose power were so great as to undo rape and bring her back from death. And every mother must have longed for the power of Demeter, the efficacy of her anger, the reconciliation with her lost self."[22]

Arnow's essentially tragic vision, then, precludes the efficacy of Demeter's power. The world of *The Dollmaker* is unmitigatedly patriarchal, dominated by husbands, the moguls of capitalism, and an Old Testament God intent on the destruction of women, children, and nature itself. Chesler's poetic projection of the fate of Demeter in modern times pertains to Arnow's novel and describes it poignantly:

And it happened as quickly as this. Demeter was stripped of her powers, torn from her maidenhood, and exiled into history as a wretched, fearful wanderer. No longer was she a mother-goddess. Now Demeter appeared only as a stepmother, often a cruel one, or as a witch, often an evil one. . . .

In our time, the stepmothers wander still—exiles, with no memory of what has gone before. Demeter has been known to curse at passing airplanes, to dress in shapeless mourning costumes, to talk to herself, to talk nonsense. . . . Often these days, when Demeter gives birth to a child, she abandons her then and there, turning her own face to the hospital wall. Sometimes, as in a trance, Demeter tries to keep her daughter at home with her again forever.[23]

The powerful Demeter is thus transformed, reduced, to Mary, the suffering figure of the *Pietá*.

Adrienne Rich has defined Margaret Atwood's *Surfacing* as "a more complex version of the Demeter-Kore myth."[24] Atwood's novel involves a reversal of the mother-daughter roles: the mother is dead, and it is the daughter who mourns her and finally recalls her, for however briefly. Yet, in that momentary vision, the protagonist has experienced an illumination which affirms, not the deification of her mother or herself, but the essential humanity of both.

Atwood's central concern is for the lost daughter, alienated from herself and from society, without identity or name, without the ability to love or feel. She is a divided woman, quite literally schizophrenic and missing a crucial part of herself. Thus, images of splitting, amputation, separation, dominate the early parts of the novel. The protagonist laments her condition, not understanding at this point what can heal her, what can make her complete:

I'd allowed myself to be cut in two. Woman sawn apart in a wooden crate, wearing a bathing suit, smiling, a trick done with mirrors, I read it in a comic book: only with me there had been an accident and I came apart. The other half, the one locked away, was the only one that could live; I was the wrong half, detached, terminal. I was nothing but a head, or, no, something minor like a severed thumb; numb. (*Surfacing*, p. 129)

Having thus committed psychological suicide, the protagonist intuits that she must somehow be reborn. As if recreating a literal birth, she returns to her childhood home in the Canadian backwoods and seeks out her parents. While her ostensible search is for her father, presumed dead or mad, "bushed" by loneliness and the confrontation with the wilderness, her spiritual search is for her dead mother. Her memories, fragments of which are constantly surfacing unbidden, center on her mother. The garden was hers and recalls memories for the protagonist of her mother feeding wild birds from her hand, keeping a journal about the weather, frightening away an intruding bear. The mother's leather jacket still hangs in the cabin: "My mother's jacket is hanging on a nail beside the window, there's nobody in it; I press my forehead against it. Leather smell, the smell of loss; irrecoverable" (p. 204).

For the protagonist, increasingly conscious of her split and inadequate self as the novel progresses, the mother becomes more and more apotheosized, losing her humanity to assume the characteristics of a nature goddess, a Demeter. The protagonist credits her mother with superhuman knowledge and powers: "My father explained everything but my mother never did which only convinced me that she had the answers but wouldn't tell" (p. 86); existing outside of time, the mother "was either ten thousand years behind the rest or fifty years ahead of them" (p. 60). Even the mother's leather jacket becomes a talisman, a saint's relic endowed with magic properties. The protagonist sees her mother as representing Nature itself: giving birth, saving life, prohibiting war and cruelty, she is a life principle, but dying herself, she contains the mysteries of death. Perhaps, the protagonist conjectures, her mother might even transcend death: "The reason they invented coffins, to lock the dead in, preserve them, they put makeup on them; they didn't want them spreading or changing into anything else. The stone with the name and the date was on them to weight them down. She would have hated it, that box, she would have tried to get out" (p. 176). Perhaps, in fact, the mother *has* transcended death; or at least the protagonist, in a desperate attempt to heal herself, has conjured her up. The mother appears in a typical pose, feeding blue jays:

Then I see her. She is standing in front of the cabin, her hand stretched out, she is wearing her gray leather jacket; her hair is long, down to her shoulders in the style of thirty years ago, before I was born; she is turned half away from me, I can see only the side of her face. She doesn't move, she is feeding them: one perches on her wrist, another on her shoulder.

I've stopped walking. At first I feel nothing except a lack of surprise: that is where she would be, she has been standing there all along. Then as I watch and it doesn't change I'm afraid it isn't real, paper doll cut by my eyes, burnt picture, if I blink she will vanish.

She must have sensed it, my fear. She turns her head quietly and looks at me, past me, as though she knows something is there but she can't quite see it. The jays cry again, they fly up from her, the shadows of their wings ripple over the ground and she's gone. (p. 213)

Yet another way that the protagonist believes she can resurrect her mother is by *becoming* her mother, giving birth to a new psychological self as well as to an infant. She fancies that her mother would have attempted to communicate with her across the barrier of death, would have left some message as to how her daughter might survive. The protagonist is mysteriously drawn to scrapbooks of her childhood drawings preserved by her mother; magically, one page feels "heavier and warmer" (p. 185). The "gift" is her own drawing of "a woman with a round moon stomach: the baby was sitting up inside her gazing out" (p. 185). Not at this point recognizing that the drawing is a depiction of her own childhood fantasy that she herself had watched the world from her mother's transparent womb, the protagonist interprets the picture as an instruction from her dead mother: "They were my guides, she had saved them for me, pictographs, I had to read their new meaning with the help of the power. The gods, their likenesses: to see them in their true shape is fatal. While you are human; but after the transformation they could be reached. First I had to immerse myself in the other language" (p. 185).

The "other language" is, of course, gibberish; in attempting to transform herself from the human in order to see the gods, the protagonist but confirms the fact that she is mad, a prisoner of her own childhood fantasies. She proceeds to follow what she believes are her mother's instructions: she must imitate her mother by becoming pregnant, assuming the aspect of the woman in the drawing, "the miraculous double-woman." Like Chesler's madwomen, the protagonist is attempting to give birth to herself. She waits until the moon is right and then leads her lover out to the lakeshore. Writes Carol P. Christ: "As she conceives, the protagonist resembles the Virgin Mother Goddesses of old: at one with nature and her sexual power, in tune with the rhythms of the moon, complete in herself, the male being incidental."[25] In an earlier book, I, too, have misunderstood Atwood's intention, having described the conception (which is only *possibly* a conception) as a cure for madness rather than a symptom, "a psychological rebirth, a healing of the divided self."[26] Atwood is too practical, too sensible, too much the existentialist for either my former psychoanalytic interpretation or Carol P. Christ's spiritual one to apply. At this point in the novel, the protagonist is still seeking out mythological roles in which to hide from her own identity, still fabricating romantic fairy tales, still acting out her sense of division and alienation. Her reenactment of the Demeter-Kore myth is as delusive as her search for the Indian gods or for Christ, as was explored in the previous chapter.

Atwood's rendition of the mother-daughter relationship in *Lady Oracle* would corroborate such an interpretation. While Joan Foster's mother is not nearly so sympathetic as the mother in *Surfacing*, she is still the subject of fantasy and myth. She is, at times, the evil queen of *Snow White*, sitting before her three-way mirror:

My mother always had a triple mirror, so she could see both sides as well as the front of her head. In the dream, as I watched, I suddenly realized that instead of three reflections she had three actual heads, which rose from her toweled shoulders on three separate necks. This didn't frighten me, as it seemed merely a confirmation of something I'd always known . . . my mother was a monster. (*Lady Oracle*, p. 70)

In another of Joan's fantasies, her mother becomes the Lady of Shallot, watching the world through a mirror: "She had been the lady in the boat, the death barge, the tragic lady with flowing hair and stricken eyes, the lady in the tower. She couldn't stand the view from the window, life was her curse" (p. 363). Joan herself has lived this particular myth, fearing to face a real world, imitating her own suicide, floating to the illusion of freedom in a death barge.

These mythologies about mothers, Atwood seems to reiterate, are essentially destructive and must be placed in perspective; only when we allow our mothers their right to human status can we achieve the same for ourselves. Joan Foster, like the protagonist of *Surfacing*, recreates her mother, brings her back from the dead, but finally begins to see the danger involved:

She'd never really let go of me because I had never let her go. It had been she standing behind me in the mirror, she was the one who was waiting around each turn, her voice whispered the words. . . . Why did I have to dream about my mother, have nightmares about her, sleepwalk out to meet her? My mother was a vortex, a dark vacuum, I would never be able to make her happy. . . . Maybe it was time for me to stop trying. (*Lady Oracle*, p. 363)

The protagonist of *Surfacing* comes to a similar realization that she and her mother are both very human women; neither is a goddess or a myth:

No total salvation, resurrection, Our father, our mother, I pray,

Reach down for me, but it won't work: they dwindle, grow, become what they were, human. Something I never gave them credit for. . . . Our mother, collecting the seasons and the weather and her children's faces, the meticulous records that allowed her to omit the other things, the pain and isolation and whatever it was she was fighting against, something in a vanished history, I can never know. They are out of reach now, they belong to themselves, more than ever. (Pp. 221–22)

Thus, Atwood's prescription for sanity seems to involve a necessity to move beyond mythology, including the myth of the Great Mother. As Atwood stated in an interview:

Would a matriarchal theology exalt women and give men a secondary place? If so, I'm not interested because it would be the same problem in reverse. It wouldn't interest me to have all the priests be women and all the altar boys be men. I'd prefer an egalitarian or human religion. Women are interested in female religious figures now simply because we've starved for them, but that doesn't mean that we should desacralize men and that women should be made sacred. There's no point in destroying a male child *instead* of a female one.[27]

Having passed beyond her need to resurrect the mother-goddess, Atwood's protagonist of *Surfacing* returns from delusion, turns the mirror so she can see her reflection, and takes a hard look at reality: "I turn the mirror around: in it there's a creature neither animal nor human, furless, only a dirty blanket, shoulders huddled over into a crouch, eyes staring blue as ice from the deep sockets; the lips move by themselves. This was the stereotype, straws in the hair, talking nonsense or not talking at all" (p. 222). Insanity itself is, for Atwood, a dangerous romance, the ultimate myth, the denial of humanity.

While the benevolent mother, whether as Demeter or as

Mary, represents one aspect of the great goddess and of female psychology, Black Kali, or the destructive mother, is another. Such ambivalence on the part of mothers is most often manifested toward sons, according to Helen Diner in *Mothers and Amazons*. Diner describes the maternal necessity to expel, finally, perhaps, to kill:

> Here lies the original conflict of maternal emotions. Like every true tragedy, it is inextinguishable in its ambivalence, beyond love and hatred, a contradiction of sentiments, because she wants to possess and to lose her son at one and the same time. As the White Mother, she wants to protect him. As the Black Mother, she expels the helpless creature. The animal mother herself bites through the umbilical cord; the Australian aborigine mother, waking and fasting, hurries the novice through the puberty rites; the mistress of the female clan ordains the law of exogamy; Thetis herself brings the suit of gilded armor to Achilles so that he can go down to certain death. They are all deeds of the Black Mother with the white, tearful face.[28]

Adrienne Rich also explores this maternal schizophrenia:

> And, at the two ends of a spectrum which is really a continuum, [the mother] is Kali, the "black mother" of Hindu religion, fangs ecstatically bared, a necklace of skulls around her neck, dancing on her dead husband's body; while in Michelangelo's white-satin-marble *Pieta* she bends her virginal mannequin's face above the icy, dandiacal corpse of the son on her lap.[29]

The paradox of the mother as both creator and killer is the focus of Toni Morrison in both *Song of Solomon* and *Sula*.

Sula, in fact, is a novel defined by religious paradox: the setting is the microcosmic Medallion, Ohio, so named, perhaps, to recall the Mantra or Jung's mandala in which all paradox is resolved. The black neighborhood of Medallion is called "the bottom," although it is actually situated on hills overlooking the white parts of town; mythologically, it is "the bottom of heaven" (*Sula*, p. 5). God himself is an enigma, his proven malevolence establishing the paradoxical truth that "the only way to avoid the Hand of God is to get in it" (p. 56). The greatest paradox, however, lies in the fact that, within Morrison's black world, women and not men order and direct the universe.

Eva, significantly named, as are all Morrison's characters, is the archetypal matriarch. She is strength and power incarnate: a one-legged woman who can read dreams and predict death, she sits in her wagon on the third floor of her house and directs the lives of those below. She even has the power to name, that ultimate power which Mary Daly says has been stolen from women since God granted Adam and not Eve the power to name the animals. Not only has Eva named her own children, but she has also named a whole variety of refugees who live in her house: a stray white man she ironically calls "Tar Baby" and three small boys, all of whom become "Dewey." Since all three, because of Eva's whimsey, share the same name, they come to share the same personality and even the same indistinguishable appearance. "What you need to tell them apart for?" Eva asks, "They's all Deweys" (p. 32). All men in Eva's matriarchal domain are thus reduced to nonidentities or infants by their very names: "Boy-boy," "Sweet Plum."

To name is to have power, and Eva's power extends from giving birth to dealing death. She loves her son, Plum; she has sacrificed even her leg to collect insurance money and provide for her children. But Plum returns from war to his mother's house a drug addict, helpless as an infant. She murders him, burns him alive in his bed, because he "wanted to crawl back in my womb": "Godhavemercy, I couldn't birth him twice. . . . I done everything I could to make him leave me and go on and live and be a man but he wouldn't and I had to keep him out so I just thought of a way he could die like a man not all scrunched up inside my womb, but like a man. . . . But I held him close first. Real close. Sweet Plum. My baby boy" (p. 62). As Eva pours the gasoline over her son before she lights the match, he feels the sensation of "some kind of baptism, some kind of blessing" (p. 40). The fire Eva lights is as paradoxical as her love: it purifies while it destroys.

Helen Diner indicates that birth itself is the initial confrontation with the "black face" of "the Great Mother":

Yes, she prepares food for the all-consuming time, nothing else. She drives defenseless babes from their beautiful protection into the irreversible, into the chain of "Never more's," and does so much too cruelly for anyone to complain. Being born means being dragged out of the small child and being imprisoned in a disgusting old thing, being pulled by one's hair and nerves in only one direction, without a respite, without pity, where happiness and duration exclude one another and any victory, no matter how hotly contested, must end in the cold defeat of lying down to die.[30]

Eva is not so violent toward her daughters as toward her son; she has, in fact, risked her own life to save her daughter Hannah from a similar death by fire. Diner explains that the maternal urge to expel "ends with the birth when it comes to the daughters. The daughters, repetitions of herself to some degree, often remain close to her for a long time, strengthening the female substance with their youth."[31] But neither is Eva demonstrative in her affection toward her daughters. A grown-up Hannah asks her mother, "Mamma, did you ever love us?" (p. 58). Eva responds that Hannah's very survival was evidence that she loved her children:

"You want me to tinkle you under the jaw and forget 'bout them sores in your mouth? Pearl was shittin' worms and I was supposed to play rang-around-the-rosie? . . ."
   "No time. They wasn't no time. Not none. Soon as I got one day

done here comes a night. With you all coughin' and me watchin' so
TB wouldn't take you off and if you was sleepin' quiet I thought, O
Lord, they dead and put my hand over your mouth to feel if the
breath was comin' what you talkin' 'bout did I love you girl I stayed
alive for you can't you get that through your thick head or what is
that between your ears, heifer?" (P. 60)

In her essay "Mothers and Daughters: Another Minority
Group," Natalie M. Rosinsky discusses "the inapplicability
of society's maternal stereotypes to women in general and
minority women in particular. Overcoming racial and
economic oppression to support her children, Eva has not
had time to channel her energies into the genteel pastimes
prescribed by mainstream culture."[32] Thus Morrison takes
the stereotype of the black culture as matriarchal and raises it
to mythic levels.

As in all matriarchal societies, according to Helen Diner[33]
and J. J. Bachofen,[34] paternity is unimportant in Morrison's
account, and polyandry, whether contemporaneous or
successive, is the norm. In Eva's matriarchal house, which
she shares with her daughter and her granddaughter Sula,
men come and go and are enjoyed sexually but are never
taken seriously. "The Peace women loved maleness, for its
own sake" (p. 35). Only at the risk of loss of power could they
love an individual male.

Sula almost commits such an error in her relationship with
Ajax. She discovers in time, however, that her failure to
learn his true name (really Albert Jacks) is a failure of her
matriarchal power. Ajax all along has remained true to a
matriarchal vision, loving his own powerful mother and the
power in Sula. He brings her bottles of milk, which he drinks
himself. He will not permit her to abdicate matriarchal
power and thus force him into responsible adulthood.

This same sort of matriarchal proclivity for polyandry
accounts for Sula's seduction of her friend's husband:

She had no thought at all of causing Nel pain when she bedded down with Jude. They had always shared the affection of other people: compared how a boy kissed, what line he used with one and then the other. Marriage, apparently, had changed all that, but having had no intimate knowledge of marriage, having lived in a house with women who thought all men available, and selected from among them with a care only for their tastes, she was ill prepared for the possessiveness of the one person she felt close to. (P. 103)

The early relationship between Nel and Sula is one defined by matriarchal values. "Nel was the first person who had been real to [Sula], whose name she knew" (p. 103). For Nel, "talking to Sula had always been a conversation with herself" (p. 82). Diner informs us that the name for "sister" in the matriarchal culture of Samoa is *tamasa*, "sacred child."[35] The sacred sisterhood of Sula and Nel is confirmed in a parody of the kind of defloration ritual which Diner describes in connection with matriarchal cultures. In the summer of their twelfth year, Nel and Sula sit beside a river, playing in the grass:

But soon [Nel] grew impatient and poked her twig rhythmically and intensely into the earth, making a small neat hole that grew deeper and wider with the least manipulation of her twig. Sula copied her, and soon each had a hole the size of a cup. Nel began a more strenuous digging and, rising to her knees, was careful to scoop out the dirt as she made her hole deeper. Together they worked until the two holes were one and the same. When the depression was the size of a small dishpan, Nel's twig broke. With a gesture of disgust she threw the pieces into the hole they had made. Sula threw hers in too. Nel saw a bottle cap and tossed it in as well. Each then looked around for more debris to throw into the hole: paper, bits of glass, butts of cigarettes, until all the small defiling things they could find were collected there. Carefully they replaced the soil and covered the entire grave with uprooted grass.

Neither one had spoken a word. (P. 50)

Immediately following these ceremonies is the ritualized sacrifice of the male-child; Chicken Little is thrown into the river and drowns.

Chicken Little's death, however, is preceded by his joy, the exaltation of flight as Sula swings him out over the water. Given a matriarchal vision, perhaps all death is but a return to the womb, a place of dark comfort. Thus the Deweys and many others in Medallion march in ecstacy into the abandoned womb-like tunnel where they are smothered to death. Sula herself dies in a fetal position, thumb in her mouth, marvelling at the comfort and peace of death: " 'Well, I'll be damned,' she thought, 'it didn't even hurt. Wait'll I tell Nel' " (p. 128).

Morrison has pursued similar themes in *Song of Solomon*. Again she presents a society of three women, three generations, dominated this time, not by one-legged Eva, but by Pilate Dead, who, presumably like the Biblical Eve, has no navel. Like Eva Peace, Pilate is a matriarch, a goddess figure superceding Christian values, as her name, Pilate, or Christ-killer, would indicate. Also like Eva, Pilate has the power to name, and to protect that power she carries her own written name in a small brass box strung through her left ear lobe. Pilate's name is, symbolically, her very soul. As she dies, a bird circles, swooping down to pluck up the shiny box which holds the written name, and flies off with it. Morrison observes, "Without ever leaving the ground, she could fly" (*Song of Solomon*, p. 340).

Always, Morrison is sympathetic to the matriarchal culture, affirming its power over the oedipal horrors of the black middle-class imitation of patriarchal social arrangements. Pilate's nephew, Milkman Dead (so nick-named because he nursed from his mother until he wore long pants), is, throughout the novel, irresistably drawn to Pilate's house and the mother-culture it represents. Pilate is, in one sense, Milkman's spiritual mother, since it was she who administered the potion to his father which resulted in his conception. In spite of the fact that Milkman abandons Pilate's beloved granddaughter, breaking her heart and driving her to suicide, Pilate forgives him and dies in his place, a victim of the violence which pervades black, patriarchal culture. When Pilate dies, Milkman laments, "There must be another one like you. . . . There's got to be at least one more woman like you" (p. 340).

Pilate dies, like Sula, a sacrificial victim. Thus Morrison's story recreates a feminist view of world history: the death of matriarchy at the hands of male violence. Yet, Morrison's novel can be understood on a psychological level as well as a mythological one. Morrison understands the complexities of the goddess psychology and its ramifications for human women. She is well aware, for example, that the myth of the black superwoman negates black women's humanity. The real political significance and the essential power of both Eva Peace and Pilate Dead can be found, not in their mythological identities, but in their common assertion of human dignity.

The feminist controversy over the goddess continues, as women writers and theologians attempt self-definition and self-affirmation. Many contemporary women novelists, like several whose works are explored in this chapter, would deny, with either regret or relief, the efficacy of the goddess. Mary, Demeter, and Kali, all aspects of one identity, are not dead, perhaps, but certainly they have been rendered powerless in much of contemporary fiction. As Chesler writes in *Women and Madness*, "Goddesses never die. They slip in and out of the world's cities, in and out of our dreams, century after century, answering to different names, dressed differently, perhaps even disguised, perhaps idle and unemployed, their official altars abandoned, their temples feared or simply forgotten."[36]

Some feminist theologians, however, do not agree with the novelists discussed or with Chesler; they prefer to think, rather, that the goddess is alive and well, a positive power if only we will recognize her. Carol P. Christ, for example, celebrates what she perceives as the presence of the goddess in all women. The following description is of Christ's visit to a contemporary "Goddess-recovery group":

Women gather in groups to pay homage to "the Goddess" by studying ancient religions, sharing personal visions and inventing new rituals. There are no official ideologies and no Scriptures. There is no magisterium. Reverence for nature, respect for the female body, and a cosmic awareness of the rhythms and energies of life are significant elements in these shared experiences. Many of these groups have revived ancient mythologies from goddess-worshipping cultures; some have consciously aligned themselves with wholesome witchcraft traditions that cultivate intuition, dreams and psychic healing.[37]

Madonna Kolbenschlag also sees the resurrection of the goddess as crucial in representing an antidote to patriarchal religious experience:

It exorcises archetypal images through a process of renominization; it overcomes transcendent instrumentality in immanence; it derationalizes religious experience through the recovery of mysticism and the "numinous"; it replaces clerical elitism with the authority of the individual; it demystifies transcendent religion by identifying divine power within natural energies.[38]

Such attempts on the part of women to recover the goddess, to find a mother figure to replace an unsympathetic male deity, are, perhaps, manifestations of an understandable anxiety in the face of a newly won freedom. As Naomi Goldenberg writes, "When a symbol as pervasive as that of the father-god begins to die, tremendous anxiety is generated. Other images arise to take its place almost immediately. Candidates for different god images are already being nominated either to replace the father-god or to provide him with a female retinue."[39]

Perhaps contemporary feminism can help to overcome women's anxiety at the loss of tradition, not, ideally, through goddess worship, but through reverence for the self and for the humanity of women in general. Historically and fictionally, the goddess, whether as Mary, Demeter or Kali, has not fared well. To resurrect her is perhaps to lose the self in mythological identities as limiting and inhibiting as those constructed by the fathers and thus to forfeit status as subject, power as political and existential agent. As Doris Lessing's protagonist of *The Golden Notebook* affirms, "The next stage is, surely, that I leave the safety of myth and Anna Wulf walks forward alone" (*Golden Notebook*, p. 470).

3
THE GARDEN

Our model is neither the romanticized primitive jungle nor the modern technological wasteland. Rather it expresses itself in a new command to learn to cultivate the garden, for the cultivation of the garden is where the powers of rational consciousness come together with the harmonies of nature in partnership.

Rosemary Radford Reuther,
"Motherearth and the Megamachine:
A Theology of Liberation in a
Feminine, Somatic and Ecological
Perspective"

The primal myth of the garden has always provided the basic metaphor for North American literature, expressing both religious sensibility and national consciousness. R. W. B. Lewis states in *The American Adam* that, for Americans of the eighteenth and nineteenth centuries, the garden metaphor "described the world as starting up again under fresh initiative, in a divinely granted second chance for the human race after the first chance had been so disastrously fumbled in the darkening Old World."[1] Of men's view of their place in the New World garden, Lewis writes: "Adam was the first, the archetypal, man. His moral position was prior to experience, and in his very newness he was fundamentally innocent. The world and history lay all before him."[2] The metaphor persisted throughout the nineteenth century and into the twentieth, the development of technology and the resulting violation of nature being perceived as a second Fall.

The same old Eve, meanwhile, waited and watched.

Women writers are now reclaiming the garden, rejecting the modern, denatured, technological world they regard as patriarchal in origin and essence. The revitalization of such romance elements is common in much contemporary fiction by men as well as women, according to Northrop Frye, who explains in *Secular Scripture* that the vision of a "pastoral, paradisal, and radically simplified form of life obviously takes on a new kind of urgency in an age of pollution and energy crisis."[3] In feminist literature, however, such images are political as well as personal. Shulamith Firestone in *The Dialectic of Sex* predicts a "hell on earth" if the mismanagement of technology continues.[4] Mary Daly warns in *Gyn/Ecology*: "Phallic myth and language generate, legitimate, and mask the material pollution that threatens to terminate all sentient life on this planet."[5] Many other contemporary feminist writers are also now exploring the connections between feminism and ecology, perceiving a link between sexual rape and the rape of the earth. In their novels, they are depicting nature in metaphoric terms as a place of escape, as sanctuary, as revelation.

According to Simone de Beauvoir, nature has always been the realm of women; the young girl, as yet unconquered in the sexual war, is especially at home there:

Empty and unlimited, she seeks from deep within her nothingness to attain All. That is why she will devote a special love to Nature: still more than the adolescent boy, she worships it. Unconquered, inhuman, Nature subsumes most clearly the totality of what exists. The adolescent girl has not as yet acquired for her use any portion of the universal: hence it is her kingdom as a whole; when she takes possession of it, she also proudly takes possession of herself.[6]

The literary education of many contemporary women writers began, undoubtedly, with Frances Hodgson Burnett's *The Secret Garden*,[7] a novel for children which depicts a young girl's discovery of nature in terms similar to those described by de Beauvoir. Burnett's Mary, like the nursery-rhyme Mary, is originally quite contrary. Ultimately she becomes a happy and mature young woman through her exploration and renovation of a locked and abandoned rose garden, an experience which she later shares with two boys and, finally, with the rest of her small world. By helping Mary in the garden, one boy is cured of a crippling disease, and he, in turn, cures his father of chronic melancholia. Thus, through Mary's efforts, the garden is unlocked and the world itself becomes a garden, redeemed and purified.

Vestiges of Burnett's story (and perhaps of Lewis Carroll's tiny and illusive rose garden as perceived by Alice) survive in many examples of contemporary literature by women. Even for the adult woman, de Beauvoir writes, nature still represents "a kingdom and a place of exile; the whole in the guise of the Other."[8]

For Annie Dillard in *Pilgrim at Tinker Creek*, nature represents a "kingdom" in every sense of the word, including its masculine connotations. Her book is not at all novelistic: we do not know why she has fled the smoke stacks of Pittsburg to live alone in a valley of Virginia's Blue Ridge Mountains—perhaps the reason is obvious. Nor can it be said that Dillard is discovering a feminist consciousness: her pronouns are inevitably masculine, and the God she discovers is unrelentingly male. Her purpose, she states, is "to keep here what Thoreau called 'a meterological journal of the

mind,' telling some tales and describing some of the sights of
this rather tamed valley, and exploring, in fear and trem-
bling, some of the unmapped dim reaches and holy fast-
nesses to which those tales and sights so dizzyingly lead."
(*Pilgrim at Tinker Creek*, p. 12).

Although the landscapes Dillard describes are frequently
very beautiful, her Eden is also a Garden of Gesthemane.
Nature is fallen, has always been so, writes Dillard, not
primarily because of man's technological pollution, but because of the nature of its creator: "Creation itself was the
fall, a burst into the thorny beauty of the real" (p. 221).
Violence is the norm, sudden death the ordinary: frogs are
sucked dry by voracious insects, their skins collapsing into
dried bags; black widows eat their husbands; praying
mantises eat their babies; "we live in a world in which half
the creatures are running from—or limping from—the
other half" (p. 239).

The very existence of death, violent or otherwise, is for
Dillard sufficient proof of a universal absurdity. Death is
"the thorn in the flesh of the world" (p. 240); people as well as
less sentient beings are subject to its vagaries: "They die
their daily death as utterly as did the frog, *people*, played
with, dabbled upon, when God knows they loved their life"
(p. 272). The author herself, a Prometheus without immortality, is "a sacrifice bound with cords to the horns of the
world's rock altar, waiting for worms" (p. 248). Even her
book, she says, is "a straying trail of blood" (p. 13). God,
whom Dillard sees as responsible for this whimsical giving
and taking of life, must therefore be a madman, "some sort of
carnival magician . . . some fast-talking worker of wonders
who has the act backwards" (p. 11). In a later book, *Holy the
Fin*, Dillard writes: "Of faith I have nothing, only of truth:
that this one God is a brute and traitor abandoning us to
time, to necessity and the engines of matter unhinged.
. . . Who will teach us to pray?" (p. 45).

In spite of such iconoclasm, however, Dillard's ultimate purpose, as surely as it was Milton's, is to justify the ways of God. Violence exists so that we may perceive beauty; death operates to give life its value. Death, therefore, is also mystical and beautiful: the rash of pellagra covering the bodies of people dead from a famine Dillard sees as "tattooed flowers . . . the roses of starvation" (*Pilgrim at Tinker Creek*, p. 272). Even violence contains a mystery which leads to revelation. Dillard opens her book with images of blood transformed to roses, the scratches left by her cat on her bare chest assuming the significance of a stigmata:

He'd stick his skull under my nose and purr, stinking of urine and blood. Some nights he kneaded my bare chest with his front paws, powerfully, arching his back, as if sharpening his claws, or pummeling a mother for milk. And some mornings I'd wake in daylight to find my body covered with paw prints in blood; I looked as though I'd been painted with roses. . . .

What blood was this, and what roses? It could have been the rose of union, the blood of murder, or the rose of beauty bare and the blood of some unspeakable sacrifice or birth. The sign on my body could have been an emblem or a stain, the keys to the kingdom or the mark of Cain. I never knew as I washed, and the blood streaked, faded, and finally disappeared, whether I'd purified myself or ruined the blood sign of the passover. We wake, if we ever wake at all, to mystery, rumors of death, beauty, violence. (Pp. 1–2)

Beauty and revelation, then, are Dillard's ultimate justification for God and death. One lives in spite of death because there are individual moments, flashes or epiphanies, during which one is permitted, like Moses, to see "the back parts of God" (p. 208), moments when "the mountains open and a new light roars in spate through the crack and the mountains slam" (p. 35). Such a moment of intense perception occurs while Dillard, unprepared, walks along the banks of Tinker Creek:

I saw the tree with the lights in it. I saw the backyard cedar where the mourning doves roost charged and transfigured, each cell buzzing with flame. I stood on the grass with the lights in it, grass that was wholly fire, utterly focused and utterly dreamed. It was less like seeing than like being for the first time seen, knocked breathless by a powerful glance. The flood of fire abated, but I'm still spending the power. (P. 35)

For Dillard at least, this is adequate compensation and sufficient justification. Her Eden, like the original garden, is governed by a male principle whose manifestations are raised to the level of grandeur. In this vision of nature, Dillard departs not only from the sentimental pastoralism of earlier American literature, but from the view held by the majority of women writers in both this century and the last. Sandra Gilbert and Susan Gubar in *The Madwoman in the Attic* state that novelistic and poetic depictions of nature by nineteenth-century women were metaphoric expressions of "yearnings for motherly or sisterly precursors," that women writers sought the "mother country," the female aspect of nature.[9] In a technological age in which women are still not trained in technology, correctly regarding it as a male domain, nature as female principle becomes an even more prominent and vital literary image.

In Sally Miller Gearhart's *The Wanderground*, for example, women and only women are permitted communion with the great mother figure that is nature. Gearhart's futuristic fantasy is based on the assumption that men have become so violent, so cruel, so dominant, that women have been forced out of the cities ruled by men. They have taken refuge in the hills and deserts outside the cities, establishing their own separate society which is primitive but superior.

The "Hill Women" make their "nests" in tree tops, hold their ritualistic celebrations beneath the benevolent and female moon, and perfect their miraculous abilities to communicate messages without language. Not only can they communicate with each other in this fashion, even over long distances, but their affinity with nature has permitted them to talk with trees, fish, animals—all of whom talk back in some sort of "rhythm of pneuma exchange" (*Wanderground*, p. 13). Even when language does contain words, these are adapted to reflect what Gearhart portrays as a supraconsciousness capable of rejecting any aspect of sexism. The women "enfold" each other rather than discuss; they "gather-stretch" rather than hold a meeting. With this emphasis on experimental language, Gearhart reiterates the messages of theologians like Daly and Kolbenschlag[10] that women must find a new language in order to exorcise from the unconscious mind the myths of patriarchy; they must claim their lost Edenic right to name. Daly writes:

One may not dare to think out loud women's words—at least, not too much. We know the penalties for that.

As a result the new sounds of free silence may be hard for many to understand. They are many-faceted. We speak forth shapes and colors, utter textures, flash forth to each other in a flow of understanding what is too awesome to be understood: our own self-birth in sisterhood. . . .

This multi-faced communication that is being born among women in the modern technological jungle of America is non-speech in the terms of our culture . . . the new sounds of silence, sparking forth a network of boundary communication, is the dawning of communal New Being. This is neither "public" nor "private," neither "objective" nor "subjective." It is intersubjective silence, the vibrations of which are too high for the patriarchal hearing mechanism. It is, then, ultrasonic.[11]

It is difficult for the reader to determine just how literally Daly intends us to accept this statement. The same is true of Gearhart's novel, not only in regard to her philosophy of language, but to her suspension of reality in general. Does she intend metaphor or prediction when she depicts her Hill Women in such a close alliance with nature that they are permitted to suspend its laws? Because, for Gearhart, women are "the only hope for earth's survival" (p. 2), having protected nature from the violation of men, they are rewarded by nature with supernatural abilities: they have great strength and physical stamina; they can ignore gravity and ride the wind; they can achieve motherhood without what Gearheart sees as the sexual pollution of the male. When a daughter is desired, which is apparently the only choice available, the women travel into the "deep cella," an underground cave where they experience the "egg-merging" with their mother earth which results in procreation.

Nature also rewards women by refusing to serve men, denying them sexual power outside the cities; even horses and other beasts of burden have revolted, refusing to carry men. Machines, when taken outside the city walls, will not operate. Gearhart perceives this as a justice long overdue. Men are, by their nature, rapists of both women and the earth. The ritual lesson learned by the young women of the Wanderground emphasizes this radical message: "It is too simple to condemn them all or to praise all of us. But for the sake of earth and all she holds, that simplicity must be our creed" (p. 2).

Gearhart's version of Eden is as totally female as Dillard's is male. While Dillard perceives nature as awesome in both its beauty and its violence, Gearhart depicts it as totally benevolent. The goddess is never vindictive, even when maligned; a young citizen of the Wanderground overhears an aged woman take the goddess to task:

How, unbelieving, Voki had stared at the old woman. "You cursed the goddess?" she said aloud. Artilidea laughing. "The goddess? Well, of course. Such as she is." . . . "Who's been dosing you up on reverence?" How, still shaken, Voki could not respond and how the old woman then laughed again. "If she's real then she needs some irreverence, doesn't she? Halved the ensconcement's winter grain, she did." Artilidea suddenly smiling but serious saying, "I'm cursing our own closedness, Voki. We should have known, could have cut and gathered sooner." How Voki had nodded, understanding something very important that day in the old woman's hut with the cold rain beating on the walls and the nanny goat bleating in the corner and her own muddy tracks forming puddles by the door. (P. 184)

Whether her novel is fantasy or prediction, Gearhart's mesage is clear: feminists must create their own separate environments. Again, one is reminded of the equally separatist philosophy of Mary Daly as she expresses it most radically in *Gyn/Ecology*: "In the light of our sisters the moon and stars we rekindle the Fore-Crones' fire. In its searing light we see through the fathers' lies of genesis and demise; we burn through the snarls of the Nothing-lovers."[12] The imaginative creation of Adamless Edens or no-man's lands, a literary tradition beginning with Charlotte Perkins Gilman's *Herland*, finds its most radical expression in such contemporary novels as Monique Wittig's *Les Guerilleres* and Joanna Russ's *The Female Man*, as well as in Gearhart's novel. In their depiction of separatist societies, these authors represent a controversial political statement. Interpreted literally, their works suggest that women opt for an alternative not commensurate with political reality. De Beauvoir warns repeatedly in *The Second Sex* against the "lure of separatism," even in the imagination.[13] Many contemporary feminist literary critics, like Nina Auerbach in *Communities of Women*, also perceive dangers in the fantasy of the feminine universe. Writes Auerbach: "The sources of power are irrefutably male, and to deny them is to deny the potential power of women's own existence."[14] Daly, in her earlier and slightly less radical treatise, *Beyond God the*

Father, perceives the benefits of the Fall as applicable to men as well as to women: "In that dreaded event, women reach for knowledge and, finding it, share it with men, so that together we can leave the delusory paradise of false consciousness and alienation."[15]

These arguments against separatism in no way seek to negate the salutory effects of the relationship between women and nature. The retreat into nature, whether it is solitary or in community with others, need not represent, as it does in Gearhart's novel, an enforced exile, a flight from society into a primitive if benevolent wilderness. Nature is a source of power as well as a refuge as Marge Piercy has depicted it in her utopian novel *Woman on the Edge of Time*. Piercy's image is not the jungle, but the cultivated garden, the union of art and nature which feeds both body and soul.

The reader's introduction to Piercy's future society is the crow of a rooster. There are flower and vegetable gardens everywhere, grazing cows, vine-covered cottages. People live in small communities, all of which are self-sufficient and self-governing, all stressing simplicity, partnership with nature, and sound ecological use of resources. Technology is not much in evidence, but it exists in order to free people from drudgery and from slavery to biology. *Brave New World*, Piercy indicates, was a man's idea of dystopia; for women in a totally nonsexist society, technological reproduction is a necessity. Luciente, a citizen of Piercy's utopian world, explains:

It was part of women's long revolution. When we were breaking all the old hierarchies. Finally there was that one thing we had to give up too. The only power we ever had, in return for no more power for anyone. The original production: the power to give birth. Because as long as we were biologically enchained, we'd never be equal. And males never would be humanized to be loving and tender. So we all became mothers. Every child has three. To break the nuclear bonding. (*Woman on the Edge of Time*, p. 105)

Piercy's imaginary children are decanted into a kind of paradise where they will be free of the stigmas of race and sex, free of guilt, or sin, or oedipal complexes, or the fear of God. God, Piercy tells us, is a patriarchal concept anyway, one of the "old archisms" to be utterly dismissed. Death is still a danger; although there exists the scientific knowledge capable of eliminating it, the community has voted to permit death, to concentrate its efforts on making life as perfect as possible.

The inhabitants of Piercy's utopia are not, strictly speaking, androgynous, although sex distinction is almost inconsequential in any aspect of life. The language is carefully constructed to avoid sex consciousness, the pronoun applying to both sexes being "per." Men can mother, even nurse babies by undergoing painless hormonal treatment to insure lactation. Piercy, at one point, depicts a bearded man tenderly holding an infant to his swollen breast. Women and men do whatever kinds of work they prefer or find necessary, and because of this, women's bodies have changed, become taller, slimmer-hipped, stronger. In the first chapters of the novel, Piercy permits us to believe that Luciente is a man. Slowly, however, breasts are revealed, the female emerges. Sex, quite simply, does not matter, even in sexual relationships. The only proscribed behavior, a matter of conscience and self-preservation, is the formation of permanent relationships, which could lead to the interjection of power.

The fault in the original garden, Piercy indicates, was the power granted to Adam over Eve. Piercy therefore feels it urgent to reject the concept of power altogether, to eliminate authority in any guise, whether in family units or in society as a whole. To illustrate her point, she juxtaposes her paradise with hell, her future Eden with a totally fallen and terrifying present. Beautiful, strong Luciente is, perhaps, only an imaginative projection, an alter ego for her doppleganger in the present, a forty-year-old Chicana named Consuelo Ramos who has survived on welfare and is now imprisoned in the violent ward of a state mental hospital. Connie's world is completely dominated by the forces of male power, psychiatrist and pimp merging identity, one as the violator of the mind, the other, of the body. Technology, in Piercy's vision of the present, has become a weapon of authority as Connie is punished for her race and her sex by the implantation of electrodes in her brain. Only on her visits to the future in the company of Luciente and in her final act of violent retaliation against the doctors can Connie escape the victimization by evil authority which dominates her mid-twentieth-century existence.

As if Piercy's portrayal of the present did not provide sufficient negative example, she also depicts an alternate and opposite future to Luciente's utopia. At one point, Connie somehow time travels to the wrong world and finds herself in a nightmare in which technology has completely perverted human existence and eliminated even the concept of nature from human consciousness. Connie's double in this world is Gildina, a scarcely human, gilded being who has never seen the sky. Rendered almost physically incapacitated by the technology which makes her into a parody of the female body, Gildina sits in her underground room watching pornographic movies and awaiting the favors of her owner, a seven-foot-tall caricature of masculinity called "Cash."

Piercy's intention in *Woman on the Edge of Time* is perhaps not so much to create Eden as to mourn the lack of it. Her utopian vision, while more practical and politically viable than many depicted in contemporary literature, is nonetheless a vision, a nostalgic trip through the values of the 1960s, a kind of summer camp for adults where the entertainment includes hallucinogens and free sex, neither of which entails responsibility or consequence. Piercy's emphasis, then, is a criticism of the real and present world. We must know and experience its fallen state before we can create a garden.

Like Piercy's utopia, the imaginary gardens in the novels of Doris Lessing are experienced only after the fall of the present political world. For Lessing, as for Piercy, knowledge precedes innocence; the symbolic snake must always be confronted before paradise can be regained.

In Lessing's earlier novels, nature is represented by the velds of Africa, vaguely forbidden and always sensual. That scene most representative of this phase in Lessing's progress toward the garden occurs in *A Proper Marriage* as Martha Quest, pregnant and acutely aware of her physical self, sheds her clothes and runs out into the pouring rain:

She almost ran into a gulf that opened under her feet. It was a pothole, gaping like a mouth, its red crumbling sides swimming with red water. Above it the long heavy grass almost met. Martha hesitated, then jumped straight in. A moment of repugnance, then she loosened deliciously in the warm rocking of the water. She stood to her knees in heavy mud, the red thick water closed below her shoulders. She looked up through the loose fronds of grass at the grey pit of the sky and heard a mutter of thunder. She was quite alone. A long swathe of grass had been beaten across the surface of the water, and around its stems trailed a jelly of frog spawn. . . . Martha allowed herself to be held upright by the mud, and lowered her hands through the resisting water to the hard dome of her stomach. There she felt the crouching infant, still moving tentatively around its prison, protected from the warm red water by half an inch of flesh. . . . Then, across the white-frothed surface of the pool, she saw an uncoiling in the wet mat of grass, and a lithe green snake moved its head this way and that, its small tongue flickering. It slid down over the red pulpy mud, and, clinging with its tail to a clutch of grass, it allowed itself to lie on the surface, swaying its vivid head just above the water. (*A Proper Marriage*, pp. 134–35)

The veld gives way to the city, and Lessing's fallen world is symbolized by the gray ruin of post–World War II London. Potholes are no longer lush pools of warm, fleshlike mud, but great pits left by exploded bombs. Physical nature, as well as human nature, is totally polluted, ruined, devastated. Lessing writes in *The Four-Gated City*:

On the walls multiplied the charts of the death factories, the poison factories, the factories that made instruments for the control of the mind, the maps of Hunger, Poverty, Riot and the rest; the atlases of poisoned air and poisoned earth and the places where bombs had been exploded under the sea, where atomic waste was sunk into the sea, where ships discharged filthy oil into the sea, where inland waters were dead or dying. (P. 398)

Even in those few pockets of "civilization" which still exist, where gardens are possible, invaders lurk. In Lessing's short story, "To Room Nineteen," the Rawlings' suburban garden by the river becomes a haunt for the devil, a place to go insane, a testimony to the failure of patriarchal religious symbolism. Susan Rawlings walks in her garden, oppressed by feelings of emptiness, convinced that her marriage, her life, is "like a snake biting its tail":

Well, one day she saw him. She was standing at the bottom of the garden, watching the river ebb past, when she raised her eyes and saw this person, or being, sitting on the white stone bench. He was looking at her, and grinning. In his hand was a long crooked stick, which he had picked off the ground, or broken off the tree above him. He was absent-mindedly, out of an absent-minded or freakish impulse of spite, using the stick to stir around in the coils of a blindworm or a grass snake (or some kind of snakelike creature:

it was whitish and unhealthy to look at, unpleasant). The snake was twisting about, flinging its coils from side to side in a kind of dance of protest against the teasing prodding stick.

Susan looked at him thinking: Who is the stranger? What is he doing in our garden? (*A Man and Two Women*, pp. 294–95)

When even the gardens are so infested with snakes and devils, the alternative, obviously, is to find "the way out of this collapsed little world and into another order of world altogether," as Lessing states in the closing paragraphs of *The Memoirs of a Survivor*. The Edenic return is possible only if one permits the present world to destroy itself, appropriately through the hypertechnology of germ warfare as in *The Four-Gated City*. The new garden, then, is populated by a few survivors of the holocaust and their children, anomalous beings with superior sensitivities and acute perception. Perhaps these children can save the world, but Lessing isn't sure even of these. As she indicates in later books, world history is an absurd and repetitious pattern involving vast cycles of destruction and renewal.

The story of paradise lost and regained and lost again is the theme of two of Lessing's volumes in the *Canopus in Argos* series: *Shikasta* and *The Sirian Experiments*. "Shikasta," in Persian, means, "the broken one," and Shikasta's history is earth's history, its demise inevitable. Human beings ultimately are not responsible for this; they have no free will, their very planet being a battleground for the Manichean struggle between the harmony of Canopus and the evil of Shammat. In *Shikasta* Lessing creates what she has described as "a new world for myself . . . a realm where the petty fates of planets, let alone individuals, are only aspects of the rivalries and interactions of the great galactic empires" (*Shikasta*, p. ix). Yet, even when Shikasta is under the rule of Shammat, at war and bent on destruction, there is a nostalgia for the garden:

Forced back and back upon herself, himself, bereft of comfort, security, knowing perhaps only hunger and cold: denuded of belief in "country," "religion," "progress"—stripped of certainties, there is no Shikastan who will not let his eyes rest on a patch of earth, perhaps no more than a patch of littered and soured soil between buildings in a slum, and think: yes, but that will come to life, there is enough power there to tear down this dreadfulness and heal all our ugliness—a couple of seasons, and it would all be alive again. . . . and in a war, a soldier watching a tank rear up over a ridge to bear down on him, will see as he dies grass, trees, a bird swerving past, and know immortality.

It is here, precisely here, that I place my emphasis. (P. 198)

The garden, for Lessing, remains only a dream on earth, its existence confined to the imaginative realm of complete fantasy in *The Marriages Between Zones Three, Four, and Five*. In Zone Three, Lessing presents us with a true pastoral idyll, a world of medieval-like castles and vast green meadows, populated by queens and shepherds, all beautiful and dressed in flowing garments. People sing a great deal and tell stories; there are no soldiers and no war. People love and make love but do not know the pain of passion. Motherhood, too, is painless, the tasks of child-rearing shared not only by fathers, but by numerous "mind-parents" as well.

The only snake in this garden, for Lessing at least, is the stultification of perfection, the boredom of innocence. Thus, Al*Ith, the queen, must save her people by herself experiencing a fall: by "falling in love" with the warrior king of Zone Four, she forfeits her innocence but consequently gains a higher level of perfection. The analogy with the Christian concept of the "fortunate fall" is self-evident: innocence does not provide the passage into paradise; the fall is a prerequisite to salvation. So Al*Ith finally earns her passage into the ethereal Zone Two through her suffering.

As is the case with the inhabitants of the original garden, Al*Ith's fall results in knowledge, which she then shares with her people. Many of Lessing's readers will agree, however, that the fall of Zone Three is not a fall into freedom. The society remains completely hierarchical, the ultimate and absolute authority resting with the invisible and unknowable "Providers," who, however benevolently, determine the course of all human events. The lack of existential freedom, then, is the real snake in all of Lessing's gardens.

More typical in the works of contemporary women writers is the association of very real gardens with very practical ideas of freedom. In the novels of Margaret Laurence and Joan Barfoot, both Canadian and therefore, perhaps, more conscious of the proximity of the wilderness than are authors from more urbanized countries, the garden is represented by the farm, a place of retreat and a vastly larger "room of one's own," where one is free to write or draw pictures or think or discover the self and its potential.

The protagonists of both authors, Morag Gunn in Laurence's *The Diviners* and Abra in Barfoot's *Abra*, realize that life in the wilderness, when not freely chosen, is no idyllic fantasy, particularly for women. Morag reflects on the lives of those who previously owned her land:

You wondered about people like the Cooper family, all those years ago. Trekking in here to take up their homestead. No roads. Bush. Hacking their way. Wagons and horses. . . . Then the people clearing the first growth of timber. . . . Women working like horses. Also probably pregnant most of the time. Baking bread in brick ovens, with a loaf in their own ovens. Looking after broods of chickens and kids. Terrible. Appalling. . . . How many women went mad? Loneliness, isolation, strain, despair, overwork, fear. Out there, the bush. In here, a silent worried worksodden man, squalling brats, an open fireplace, and would the shack catch fire this week or next. In winter, snow up to your thighs. A wonder they weren't all raving lunatics. Probably many were. It's the full of the moon, George—Mrs. Cooper always howls like this at such a time. (*The Diviners*, p. 77)

Barfoot's Abra is also grimly aware of the fate of her predecessors: poverty, overwork, hunger, failure, and finally, murder and suicide.

Laurence's protagonist is no pioneer; she has a telephone and a refrigerator; she lets her garden go to seed. Morag is a writer and a watcher; for her the garden is a life source for the spirit and not the body:

The small cedars, spearing lightly featheringly upwards. The fenced-off patch, where once Sarah Cooper had begun a vegetable garden all those years ago. Now it had gone to wild high seed-headed grasses, what a variety, must be dozens. And purple thistles, regal, giant. And those flowers like pale yellow snapdragons. . . . And in late summer, the goldenrod. . . . Morag regarded it as a garden of amazing splendours, in which God did all the work. . . . Like the Garden of Eden. (*Diviners*, p. 138)

Morag's life has been one of poverty and frustration, the material of realism. Yet, her sojourn in the country has led her to apprehend the mystical, to believe in magic. The title of Laurence's novel might well have been inspired by de Beauvoir's comparison of the erotic and magic powers of nature to the mysterious efficacy of the diviner's rod: "Woman's mentality perpetuates that of agricultural civilizations which worshipped the magic powers of the land: she believes in magic. Her passive eroticism makes desire seem to her not will and aggression but an attraction akin to that which causes the divining rod to dip; the mere presence of her flesh swells and erects the male's sex; why should not hidden water make the hazel rod quiver?"[16] As Morag reflects on her former life lived in cities, she wonders if her present situation is not an escape, a flight from reality and commitment. Perhaps she is "trapped in a garden of the mind, a place which no longer has a being in external reality" (p. 185). She should have raised her daughter in cities, she thinks, where she would have learned "about the survival tactics in a world now largely dedicated to Death, Slavery and the Pursuit of Unhappiness. Instead, I've made an island" (p. 292). One of Morag's novels, written here in the country, is entitled *Prospero's Daughter* and is a re-telling of *The Tempest*. Morag ultimately concludes, how-ever, that gardens of the mind and islands "in the head" are totally and inevitably necessary: "All this, the river and the willows and the gronk-gronk-gronk of the mini-dinosaur bullfrogs, it may be a fantasy. But I can bear to live here, until I die, and I couldn't elsewhere" (p. 292). Significantly, Morag's last finished novel is entitled *Shadow of Eden*.

The garden in Barfoot's novel is quite a different image. Abra, like Morag, has left a city life and a city husband, but her motive is purely the preservation of her sanity. She does not plan to write or paint, although she later does so, but wants only to escape what has become for her an insufferable life as wife and mother. She buys her farm as an alternative to suicide and her psychological survival depends on her compulsive physical labor as she wrests a garden from the wilderness. The creation of order, in nature and in her own mind, is essential. The garden becomes, she says, "the centre of my life" (*Abra*, p. 25).

So self-sufficient does Abra become during her years in the garden that even mythology loses its efficacy: the sym-bolic snake is merely an earthworm; the fall is not a threat:

An earthworm, dislodged by my rootings in the garden, coiled on the surface, gleaming, moving disjointedly and slowly, com-prehending the air and the light, its head occasionally moving, snake-like, upwards, turning slowly, tasting the atmosphere, deciding somewhere in its instincts that it was not right, not home, and turning again to descend back into the earth, calmly, without panic, moving away down into the cool moisture where it belonged, and all the time I watched. (P. 137)

Traditional religious mythology is thus rendered obsolete, but Abra's solitary life on the farm leads her to realizations which might be seen as religious, perhaps mystical: "I recalled lethargy, inertia and unease, but could not grasp them. They belonged to someone else. Here was energy, sensation, the beginning, perhaps of understanding. The beginning, perhaps, of faith? Or belief?" (p. 110).

Although Barfoot entertains the possibility that she has permitted her protagonist to withdraw from responsibility into a dream world, Abra herself never draws this conclusion. Life in the garden is simply a healing process, the antidote to a former schizophrenic existence: "It was another leap, taking perhaps years, before the idea of separation I had within myself ended and I was a unit, body, mind and the other part that may be what is called a 'soul' " (p. 134). Yet, the basic ambiguity in this novel, which Barfoot does not resolve, lies in the fact that Abra has merged herself so completely with her land that she is incapable of separating herself from it. She does not recognize and cannot talk to the daughter she deserted years before. She cannot, in the tradition of religious heroes, return as lawgiver to society. Rather, she remains "part of the wilderness, inseparable from it" (p. 107). Total alienation, then, is the price of her survival.

This problem of alienation is central for the novelist who depicts a return to the garden. Leo Marx, in his exploration of the garden image in American literature, concludes that the myth as it has been rendered in our culture has been perverted, reduced to irony:

Our inherited symbols of order and beauty have been divested of meaning. It compels us to recognize that the aspirations once represented by the symbol of an ideal landscape have not, and probably cannot, be embodied in our traditional institutions. It means that an inspiriting vision of a humane community has been reduced to a token of individual survival. The outcome of *Walden*, *Moby Dick*, and *Huckleberry Finn* is repeated in the typical modern version of the fable; in the end the American hero is either dead or totally alienated from society, alone and powerless, like the evicted shepherd of Virgil's eclogue. And if, at the same time, he pays a tribute to the image of a green landscape, it is likely to be ironic. The resolutions of our pastoral fables are unsatisfactory because the old symbol of reconciliation is obsolete.[17]

The exception to Marx's general truth is Margaret Atwood's *Surfacing*, a novel which explores the possibilities of alienation and rejects them in favor of reconciliation. Atwood's protagonist searches out her private garden in the Canadian wilderness, finds there a source of strength, and returns to the city, willing for the first time in her life to cope with civilization. Unlike the majority of fictional protagonists discussed in this chapter, Atwood's heroine does not lose herself in the garden, but completes the archetypal pattern of retreat, renewal, and return. For this reason, Francine du Plessix Gray has called her "the heroine of the thousand faces"[18] after Joseph Campbell's study of the archetypal religious hero.[19]

Atwood's vision of nature does not fit the traditional sentimental rendition of past American fiction; she does not deal in the pastoral mode. Like Annie Dillard, Atwood's protagonist recognizes the violence along with the beauty, the presence of death with that of life. This very recognition insures her survival on a practical level as she fishes for food, builds fires, makes her way through the forest, and protects her male companions in a reversal of the stereotypical male-female roles. Unlike Dillard and the majority of other contemporary writers, however, Atwood goes beyond the image of nature as place or atmosphere; in *Surfacing*, nature also becomes a metaphor for the self and its subconscious existence.

The protagonist associates this particular wilderness with her childhood; her conscious memories are here as well as those experiences that have been repressed, reinterpreted, revised. Until she confronts these memories, distinguishes fact from delusion, she remains locked within her childhood, unable to gain her passage into maturity and a sense of her own identity. As occurs in the psychoanalytic process, the protagonist must immerse herself in her self in order to find that self.

The adult protagonist is, for example, haunted by a variety of fears, only some of which have a rational basis, like those involving the abuse of technology: the dangers of the birth control pill which turns women into "chemical slot machines" (*Surfacing*, p. 96), the encroachment of pollution into the forests, the flooding of her father's land to create a dam. Her other fears, those which truly permeate her unconscious mind, are primitive and terrifying, like those experienced by children. Cameras, for example, might "steal the soul" (p. 128), as the Indians believed; they are in a class with flush toilets, things that children fear will make them disappear. She is still terrified by the idea of Jesus, the "dead man in the sky watching everything I did" (p. 52), and so continues her childhood practice of perceiving all things as imbued with magical power or religious significance. Her anxieties about her present search for her missing father also have their basis in childhood games and childhood fears: "It's like the times he used to play hide and seek with us in the semi-dark after supper, it was different from playing in a house, the space to hide in was endless; even when we knew which tree he had gone behind there was the fear that what would come out when you called would be someone else" (p. 58). The protagonist's frequent references to amputation of parts of the body are images which describe her adult feelings of alienation, of being psychologically split, but these too have their basis in anxieties quite common to children who then act them out in games: "At school they used to play a joke, they would bring little boxes with cotton wool in them and a hole cut in the bottom; they would poke their finger through the hole and pretend it was a dead finger" (pp. 129–30).

In order to overcome such anxieties and move toward adulthood, the protagonist must identify and even reexperience those feelings and events in her childhood that led to her present psychological inadequacies. Her journey home to the wilderness is an immersion in her own childhood, in the primitive jungle of her own mind. She dives repeatedly into the icy glacial lake; she moves through the forest. In the last stages of this discovery process, she prowls through the woods on all fours, eats wild berries, kicks dirt over her droppings like an animal, goes naked wrapped in a blanket only "until the fur grows." Finally, her experience is prenatal, a complete and utter loss of identity: she lies naked in the womblike lake, submerging herself until "everything is made of water." She is no longer human or even animal; but rather, she is "the thing in which the trees and animals move and grow, I am a place" (p. 213). Human concerns like language are obsolete: "the animals have no need for speech, why talk when you are a word" (p. 212).

The protagonist's return to sanity and to human existence is marked by her recognition that she must have food and shelter to survive, that she is neither animal nor primitive god and is therefore incapable of living alone in the wilderness. To live, she decides, is a responsibility to her parents, to society, to herself: "to prefer life, I owe them that" (p. 220). Language is also a human necessity, and she must "have someone to speak to and words that can be understood" (p. 222).

In returning her protagonist to the city and in effecting her reconciliation with society, Atwood does not deny the efficacy of nature. Neither, however, does she advocate some primal return, some permanent merging of womanhood with the wilderness, as some of Atwood's critics have maintained. Her argument is not, after all, for the acceptance and celebration of female biological necessity, as Carol P. Christ has suggested: "The emergence of a powerful vision of women's connection to nature in a novel of women's spiritual quest seems to suggest that women can achieve power through the acceptance of female biological roles. The traditional identification of women and nature that has been a legacy of oppression can also be a potential source of power and vision."[20] Nor can Atwood be said to share Adrienne Rich's view on the physical nature of women: "Patriarchal thought has limited female biology to its own narrow specifications. The feminist vision has recoiled from female biology for these reasons; it will, I believe, come to view our physicality as a resource, rather than a destiny."[21]

For Atwood, the metaphoric garden and nature in general are not answers, ends in themselves, but rather agents in the human confrontation with existence. Her protagonist would not choose to remain in that world of dangerous swamps, towering pine trees, and impenetrable thickets any more than she would choose to remain a prisoner of the mental chaos that is insanity. In her rendition of nature, however, Atwood has achieved that quality that de Beauvoir found so rare in women writers: "Few indeed there are who face nature in its nonhuman freedom, who attempt to decipher its foreign meanings, and who lose themselves in order to make union with this other presence."[22] Even fewer are those who return after having done so.

Another powerful incarnation of the garden occurs in Alice Walker's essay "In Search of Our Mothers' Gardens." The garden here serves as an obvious metaphor for art and is an expression of beauty and control:

My mother adorned with flowers whatever shabby house we were forced to live in. And not just your typical straggly country stand of zinnias, either. She planted ambitious gardens—and still does—with over fifty different varieties of plants that bloom profusely from early March until late November. . . .

Whatever she planted grew as if by magic, and her fame as a grower of flowers spread over three counties. Because of her creativity with her flowers, even my memories of poverty are seen through a screen of blooms—sunflowers, petunias, roses, dahlias, forsythia, spirea, delphiniums, verbena . . . and on and on.

. . . Whatever rocky soil she landed on, she turned into a garden. A garden so brilliant with colors, so original in design, so magnificent with life and creativity, that to this day people drive by our house in Georgia—perfect strangers and imperfect strangers—and ask to stand or walk among my mother's art.

I notice that it is only when my mother is working in her flowers that she is radiant, almost to the point of being invisible—except as Creator: hand and eye. She is involved in work her soul must have. Ordering the universe in the image of her personal conception of Beauty.

Her face, as she prepares the Art that is her gift, is a legacy of respect she leaves to me, for all that illuminates and cherishes life. She has handed down respect for the possibilities—and the will to grasp them. [23]

Walker would agree, I think, with Rosemary Radford Reuther as she is quoted at the beginning of this chapter: women must "cultivate the garden"; [24] we must move from romance to rational consciousness, from innocence to maturity, from victimization to power, from Eden into the world.

CONCLUSION: EVE

*My dear Julia, we've chosen to be free women, and
this is the price we pay, that's all.*
Doris Lessing, The Golden Notebook

Eve is, of course, the prototypical scapegoat traditionally
blamed for the fall of humanity, bearer of the gynephobia of
the ages. Created as an afterthought to be Adam's helpmeet,
she is a mere tenant in the Biblical garden. While representing prelapsarian innocence and obedience, she is also
the temptress, the carnal aspect of woman. Simone de
Beauvoir described her as the male projection of the ideal
woman:

Woman thus seems to be the inessential who never goes back to
being the essential, to be the absolute Other, without reciprocity.
This conviction is dear to the male, and every creation myth has
expressed it, among others the legend of Genesis, which, through
Christianity, has been kept alive in Western civilization. Eve was
not fashioned at the same time as the man; she was not fabricated
from a different substance, nor of the same clay as was used to
model Adam: she was taken from the flank of the first male. Not
even her birth was independent; God did not spontaneously choose
to create her as an end in herself and in order to be worshipped
directly by her in return for it. She was destined by Him for man; it
was to rescue Adam from loneliness that He gave her to him, in her
mate was her origin and her purpose; she was his complement on
the order of the inessential. Thus she appeared in the guise of

priviliged prey. She was nature elevated to transparency of consciousness; she was a conscious being, but naturally submissive. And therein lies the wondrous hope that man has often put in woman: he hopes to fulfill himself as a being by carnally possessing a being, but at the same time confirming his sense of freedom through the docility of a free person. No man would consent to be a woman, but every man wants women to exist.[1]

In short, no mythological figure could be more clearly antipathetic to the modern feminist consciousness than Eve. Most contemporary feminist theologians have thus dismissed Eve as a viable symbol for women and have chosen instead to celebrate Lilith, Eve's predecessor as Adam's wife. Judith Plaskow, for example, sees Lilith's rebellion against God and Adam as the archetypal paradigm for the contemporary women's movement. Plaskow "re-mythologizes" the Book of Genesis in the following way:

One day, after many months of strange and disturbing thoughts, Eve, wandering around the edge of the garden, noticed a young apple tree she and Adam had planted, and saw that one of its branches stretched over the garden wall. Spontaneously, she tried to climb it, and struggling to the top, swung herself over the wall.

She did not wander long on the other side before she met the one she had come to find, for Lilith was waiting. At first sight of her, Eve remembered the tales of Adam and was frightened, but Lilith understood and greeted her kindly. "Who are you?" they asked each other. "What is your story?" and they sat and spoke together, of the past and then of the future. They talked for many hours, not once, but many times. They taught each other many things, and told each other stories, and laughed together, and cried, over and over, till the bond of sisterhood grew between them. . . .

And God and Adam were expectant and afraid the day Eve and Lilith returned to the garden, bursting with possibilities, ready to rebuild it together.[2]

Feminist literary critics, too, have seen the figure of Lilith as representative of the assertive woman, heroic in her rebellion. Sandra Gilbert and Susan Gubar, in *The Madwoman in the Attic*, depict Lilith as the "archetypal woman creator" and a symbol for female authority:

What her history suggests is that in patriarchal culture, female speech and female "presumption"—that is, angry revolt against male domination—are inextricably linked and inevitably daemonic. Excluded from the human community, even from the semidivine communal chronicles of the Bible, the figure of Lilith represents the price women have been told they must pay for attempting to define themselves.[3]

Eve and Lilith are thus seen to form a continuum in which contemporary women are at the center, torn between the two conflicting necessities of submission and rebellion. Lilith, on the one hand, is impotent, as Plaskow, for one, recognizes: "Lilith by herself is in exile and can do nothing."[4] Eve, at least at that moment at which she leaves the garden for the world, the state of innocence for one of responsibility, offers a third alternative, which is confrontation and freedom.

In *Beyond God the Father*, Mary Daly devotes a chapter to "the exorcism of evil from Eve," defending her fall as "a Fall *into* the sacred."[5] Daly thus perceives the figure of Eve as a precursor of the benevolent Antichrist embodied in the contemporary women's movement. We might, however, prefer to interpret Eve in her essential humanity as the truly existential woman. Without either God or the Great Mother as sympathetic agent, her loneliness is terrible, and yet she chooses to claim both knowledge and freedom, regardless of price. Her confrontation is with reality: life and inevitable death.

But the faces of Eve, as they appear in contemporary fiction, are too often turned away from the existential confrontation. Freedom is more often sought in illusion and in romance than in reality; it becomes, as Patricia Meyer Spacks has written in *The Female Imagination*, "a triumph over actuality,"[6] the search being a process of avoidance rather than of confrontation. That closest approximation of the archetypal Eve in American literature, Edna Pontellier of Kate Chopin's *The Awakening*, drowns herself on the brink of freedom. As Judith Fryer writes in *The Faces of Eve*, "Edna chooses to die because it is the one, the ultimate act of free will open to her through which she can elude those who would drag her down. In becoming one with the sea she is free. She has achieved a kind of rebirth. Edna Pontellier is not a tragic heroine; she is not a fairy-tale princess. She is a woman, a real woman living in a world which has no place for her."[7]

For Doris Lessing in *The Four-Gated City*, freedom lies in madness. In Lessing's "To Room Nineteen" (in *A Man and Two Women*), the protagonist leaves a garden only to embark on a dark river that is suicide. In the novels of other contemporary writers too numerous to mention, the struggle *toward* freedom is documented, but the confrontation with its reality is avoided; we are all familiar with the ambiguous nonending, the open-road conclusion, the lack of resolution, the failure of a vision of freedom. Spacks has written: "Freedom is only a word, its implications always contradicted by reality, and the idea of a free woman is illusory as that of a free society. To make freedom a fact is the central effort of all political struggle."[8] Spacks later concludes: "The condition that makes ultimate freedom impossible is the human condition, the same for men and women."[9] Freedom, then, Spacks states, is possible only in the imagination and in the creative process.

In existential terms, however, personal freedom leading to political freedom lies, not in avoidance, but in confrontation with reality, no matter how absurd that reality may be.

Simone de Beauvoir concludes *The Second Sex* with the assertion that one must "establish the reign of liberty in the midst of the world of the given."[10] The lie, says Margaret Atwood's protagonist of *Surfacing*, "was always more disastrous than the truth would have been" (*Surfacing*, pp. 222–23).

Truth, in Atwood's terms, is the basis of freedom, which in itself is no sacred absolute but rather the declaration of identity as an autonomous self. Atwood's protagonist, then, is *most* free, not while she wanders "on all fours" through the forest, not when she surrenders identity in madness, but at the moment of her return, which is her confrontation with the truth of an absurd reality. She *chooses* to rejoin society although she perceives its dangers; she chooses to affirm human and sexual relationships although she recognizes the inevitability of failures. Her lover is "a mediator, an ambassador, offering me something"; her love for him is

useless as a third eye or a possibility. If I go with him we will have to talk, wooden houses are obsolete, we can no longer live in spurious peace by avoiding each other, the way it was before, we will have to begin. For us it's necessary, the intercession of words; and we will probably fail, sooner or later, more or less painfully. That's normal, it's the way it happens now and I don't know whether it's worth it or even if I can depend on him. . . .

To trust is to let go. I tense forward, toward the demands and questions. (*Surfacing*, p. 224)

The protagonist makes this choice in the full recognition of her existential loneliness, with the realization that there are no gods to help her, "no total salvation, resurrection" (p. 221). Atwood concludes her novel, then, at this moment of heroism, her protagonist, like Eve leaving the garden, opting not for "captivity in any of its forms," but rather for "a new freedom" (p. 224).

Another example of the "free woman" in contemporary literature is Margaret Drabble's Frances Wingate, protagonist of *The Realms of Gold*. She is a respected archeologist, a discoverer of lost desert cities; she is also the single parent of four children and mother figure to numerous other people, including her weaker lover. She is powerful because she *claims* power; her ability or condition is as amazing to her as it is to Drabble's readers:

I must be mad, she thought to herself. I imagine a city, and it exists. If I hadn't imagined it, it wouldn't have existed. All her life, things had been like that. She had imagined herself doing well at school, and had done well. Marrying, and had married. Bearing children, and had borne them. Being rich, and had become rich. Being free, and was free. Finding true love, and had found it. Losing it, and had lost it. What next should she imagine? What terrifying enormity should she next conjure forth? Should she dig again in the desert and uncover gold? Should she plant down her foot and let water spring from the dry land? Should she wave her arm and let the rocks blossom? (*Realms of Gold*, p. 31)

Drabble's point is that power and freedom must be claimed, taken; they are not gifts but the result of an exercise of will. The other members of Frances Wingate's family are all alcoholics, suicides, failures, recluses, or lunatics. Any one of them would be easy, tempting, to imitate, but she wills herself to overcome the temptation: "Always, the struggling back, the drying of eyes, the reassembling of parts" (p. 10). Even the deaths of people she loves cannot destroy her, nor can the recognition of her own inevitable death: "If one can salvage one moment from the sentence of death let us do so, let us catch at it, for we owe it to the dead, to the others, and it is all the living and the lucky can do for the dead, all they can do, given the chance, is to rejoice: overcome with joy she lay there" (p. 345).

A tremendous life force and an affirmation of the self are

Frances Wingate's secrets for survival. She is not so much an idealized figure as she is a practical role model, a real and possible alternative. She is no tragic heroine torn between the two conflicting necessities of Eve and Lilith, submission and rebellion; rather, she offers us a third choice, which is autonomy and power.

Eve, then, also is a role model: not while she is in the garden, innocent and submissive, nor yet even at the moment of rebellion when she picks the fruit. Her real heroism is evident only at that point of her exit from the garden and her confrontation with freedom. We recognize her, then, not as Other or Antichrist, not as the goddess or the myth figure—but as ourselves.

Notes
Bibliography
Index

NOTES

INTRODUCTION

1 Elizabeth Cady Stanton, *The Woman's Bible* (1895; reprint, New York: Arno Press, 1974).

2 Charlotte Perkins Gilman, *His Religion and Hers: A Study of the Faith of Our Fathers and the Work of Our Mothers* (1923; reprint, Westport, Conn.: Hyperion Press, 1976).

3 Simone de Beauvoir, *The Second Sex*, trans. H. M. Parshley (New York: Bantam, 1961), p. 669.

4 Carol P. Christ, *Diving Deep and Surfacing: Women Writers on Spiritual Quest* (Boston: Beacon Press, 1980), p. 131.

5 Adrienne Rich, *Of Woman Born: Motherhood as Experience and Institution* (New York: Bantam, 1977), p. 51.

6 De Beauvoir, *The Second Sex*, p. 585.

7 Ibid.

8 Jean Houston, "Re-seeding America: The American Psyche as a Garden of Delights," *Journal of Humanistic Psychology* 18, no. 1 (Winter 1978): 78.

9 Mary Daly, *Beyond God the Father: Toward a Philosophy of Women's Liberation* (Boston: Beacon Press, 1974), p. 73.

10 Elizabeth Gould Davis, *The First Sex* (New York: Putnam, 1971).

11 Daly, *Beyond God the Father*, p. 8.

CHAPTER 1. CHRIST

1 Theodore Ziolkowski, *Fictional Transfigurations of Jesus* (Princeton: Princeton University Press, 1972).

2 Simone de Beauvoir, *The Second Sex*, trans. H. M. Parshley (New York: Bantam, 1961), p. 636.

3 Phyllis Chesler, *Women and Madness* (New York: Avon, 1972), p. 31.

4 See Gary Lane, ed., *Sylvia Plath: New Views on the Poetry* (Baltimore: Johns Hopkins University Press, 1979).

5 All citations to the fiction discussed are in the text and refer to the editions noted in the Bibliography.

6 Ziolkowski, *Fictional Transfigurations*, p. 294.

7 This interview with Arnow took place in 1975 in Ann Arbor, Michigan.

8 Ziolkowski, *Fictional Transfigurations*, p. 294.

9 Ibid., p. 286.

10 Mary Daly, *Beyond God the Father: Toward a Philosophy of Women's Liberation* (Boston: Beacon Press, 1973), p. 60.

11 Ziolkowski, *Fictional Transfigurations*, p. 293.

12 De Beauvoir discusses similar examples of self-mutilation in young girls: "These sado-masochistic performances are at once an anticipation of the sexual experience and a protest against it; in passing these tests, one becomes hardened for all possible ordeals and reduces their harshness, including the ordeal of the wedding night. When she puts a snail on her breast, swallows a bottle of aspirin tablets, wounds herself, the young girl is hurling defiance at her future lover—'you will never inflict on me anything more hateful than I inflict on myself.' These are proud and sullen gestures of initiation to the sexual adventure" (*The Second Sex*, pp. 331–32).

13 Ursula Le Guin, "The Ones Who Walk Away from Omelas," in *The Winds' Twelve Corners* (New York: Bantam, 1976).

14 Ziolkowski, *Fictional Transfigurations*, p. 298.

15 Carol P. Christ, *Diving Deep and Surfacing: Women Writers on Spiritual Quest* (Boston: Beacon Press, 1980).

16 Francine du Plessix Gray, "Nature as Nunnery," *New York Times Book Review*, July 17, 1977, p. 3.

17 Margaret Atwood, *Survival: A Thematic Guide to Canadian Literature* (Toronto: House of Anansi Press, 1972), pp. 84–85.

18 Graeme Gibson, *Eleven Canadian Novelists* (Toronto: House of Anansi Press, 1973), p. 22.

19 Carol P. Christ, *Diving Deep and Surfacing.*

20 Barbara Hill Rigney, *Madness and Sexual Politics in the Feminist Novel: Studies in Bronte, Woolf, Lessing, and Atwood* (Madison: University of Wisconsin Press, 1978).

21 Ziolkowski, *Fictional Transfigurations*, p. 294.

22 Madonna Kolbenschlag, *Kiss Sleeping Beauty Good-Bye: Breaking the Spell of Feminine Myths and Models* (New York: Doubleday, 1979), p. 163.

23 Rita Rice, unpublished journal, Ohio State University, 1980.

24 Daly, *Beyond God the Father*, p. 96.

25 Flannery O'Connor, "Wise Blood," in *Three by Flannery O'Connor* (New York: Signet, 1962).

CHAPTER 2. MARY

1 Phyllis Chesler, *Women and Madness*, (New York: Avon, 1972), p. 28.

2 Naomi Goldenberg, *The Changing of the Gods: Feminism and the End of Traditional Religions* (Boston: Beacon Press, 1979), p. 75.

3 Simone de Beauvoir, *The Second Sex*, trans. H. M. Parshley (New York: Bantam, 1961), p. 637.

4 Mary Daly, *Beyond God the Father: Toward a Philosophy of Women's Liberation* (Boston: Beacon Press, 1973), p. 62.

5 Marina Warner, *Alone of All Her Sex: The Myth and the Cult of the Virgin Mary* (New York: Pocket Books, 1976), p. 336.

6 Ibid., p. 338.

7 Margaret Fuller, *Woman in the Nineteenth Century* (New York: Norton, 1971), p. 156.

8 De Beauvoir, *The Second Sex*, pp. 635–36.

9 Daly, *Beyond God the Father*, p. 102.

10 De Beauvoir, *The Second Sex*, p. 635.

11 Warner, *Alone of All Her Sex*, p. 71.

12 Daly, *Beyond God the Father*, p. 6.

13 Lee Anne Schreiber, "A Talk with Mary Gordon," *New York Times Book Review*, February 15, 1981, p. 26.

14 Ibid.

15 Rosemary Radford Reuther, *New Woman, New Earth: Sexist Ideologies and Human Liberation* (New York: Seabury Press, 1975), p. 58.

16 Warner, *Alone of All Her Sex*, p. 338.

17 Daly, *Beyond God the Father*, p. 90.

18 Ibid., p. 96.

19 Elizabeth Gould Davis, *The First Sex* (New York: Putnam, 1971), p. 246.

20 Madonna Kolbenschlag, *Kiss Sleeping Beauty Good-Bye: Breaking the Spell of Feminine Myths and Models* (New York: Doubleday, 1979), p. 201.

21 Adrienne Rich, *Of Woman Born: Motherhood as Experience and Institution* (New York: Bantam, 1972), p. 240.

22 Ibid., p. 243.

23 Chesler, *Women and Madness*, p. xix.

24 Rich, *Of Woman Born*, p. 243.

25 Carol P. Christ, "Margaret Atwood: The Surfacing of Women's Spiritual Quest and Vision," *Signs: A Journal of Women in Culture and Society* 2, no. 2 (Winter 1976): 323.

26 Barbara Hill Rigney, *Madness and Sexual Politics in the Feminist Novel: Studies in Bronte, Woolf, Lessing, and Atwood* (Madison: University of Wisconsin Press, 1978), p. 110.

27 Karla Hammond, "An Interview with Margaret Atwood," *American Poetry Review* 8, no. 5 (September–October 1979): 29.

28 Helen Diner, *Mothers and Amazons: The First Feminine History of Culture* (New York: Anchor, 1973), p. 87.

29 Rich, *Of Woman Born*, p. 185.

30 Diner, *Mothers and Amazons*, pp. 13–14.

31 Ibid., pp. 86–87.

32 Natalie M. Rosinsky, "Mothers and Daughters: Another Minority Group," in *The Lost Tradition: Mothers and Daughters in Literature*, ed. Cathy N. Davidson and E. M. Broner (New York: Ungar, 1980), p. 283.

33 Diner, *Mothers and Amazons*, p. 112.

34 J. J. Bachofen, *Myth, Religion, and Mother Right*, trans. Ralph Manheim (Princeton: Princeton University Press, 1967).

35 Diner, *Mothers and Amazons*, p. 61.

36 Chesler, *Women and Madness*, p. xviii.

37 Carol P. Christ, "The New Feminist Theology: A Review of the Literature," *Religious Studies Review* 3, no. 4 (October 1977): 211.

38 Kolbenschlag, *Kiss Sleeping Beauty Good-Bye*, pp. 188–89.

39 Goldenberg, *Changing of the Gods*, p. 72.

CHAPTER 3. THE GARDEN

1 R. W. B. Lewis, *The American Adam: Innocence, Tragedy, and Tradition in the Nineteenth Century* (Chicago: University of Chicago Press, 1955), p. 5.

2 Ibid.

3 Northrop Frye, *Secular Scripture: A Study of the Structure of Romance* (Cambridge: Harvard University Press, 1976), p. 149.

4 Shulamith Firestone, *The Dialectic of Sex: The Case for a Feminist Revolution* (New York: Bantam, 1971), p. 242.

5 Mary Daly, *Gyn/Ecology: The Metaethics of Radical Feminism* (Boston: Beacon Press, 1978), p. 9.

6 Simone de Beauvoir, *The Second Sex*, trans. H. M. Parshley (New York: Bantam, 1961), p. 339.

7 Frances Hodgson Burnett, *The Secret Garden* (New York: Dell, 1975)

8 De Beauvoir, *The Second Sex*, p. 669.

9 Sandra Gilbert and Susan Gubar, *The Madwoman in the Attic: The Woman Writer and the Nineteenth-Century Literary Imagination* (New Haven: Yale University Press, 1979), p. 100.

10 Madonna Kolbenschlag, *Kiss Sleeping Beauty Good-Bye: Breaking the Spell of Feminine Myths and Models* (New York: Doubleday, 1979).

11 Mary Daly, *Beyond God the Father: Toward a Philosophy of Women's Liberation* (Boston: Beacon Press, 1973), pp. 151–53.

12 Daly, *Gyn/Ecology*, p. 424

13 De Beauvoir, *The Second Sex*, p. 581.

14 Nina Auerbach, *Communities of Women: An Idea in Fiction* (Cambridge: Harvard University Press, 1978), p. 183.

15 Daly, *Beyond God the Father*, p. 67.

16 De Beauvoir, *The Second Sex*, pp. 563–64.

17 Leo Marx, *The Machine in the Garden: Technology and the Pastoral Ideal in America* (New York: Oxford University Press, 1964), p. 364.

18 Francine du Plessix Gray, "Nature as Nunnery," *New York Times Book Review*, July 17, 1977, p. 3.

19 Joseph Campbell, *Hero with a Thousand Faces* (New York: Meridian, 1956).

20 Carol P. Christ, *Diving Deep and Surfacing: Women Writers and Spiritual Quest* (Boston: Beacon Press, 1980), p. 52.

21 Adrienne Rich, *Of Woman Born: Motherhood as Experience and Institution* (New York: Bantam, 1972), p. 21.

22 De Beauvoir, *The Second Sex*, p. 669.

23 Alice Walker, "In Search of Our Mothers' Gardens," in *Working It Out*, ed. Sara Ruddick and Pamela Daniels (New York: Pantheon, 1977), pp. 92–102.

24 Rosemary Radford Reuther, "Motherearth and the Megamachine: A Theology of Liberation in a Feminine, Somatic, and Ecological Perspective," in *Womanspirit Rising: A Feminist Reader in Religion*, ed. Carol P. Christ and Judith Plaskow (San Francisco: Harper & Row, 1979), p. 52.

CONCLUSION. EVE

1 Simone de Beauvoir, *The Second Sex*, trans. H. M. Parshley (New York: Bantam, 1961), p. 131.

2 Judith Plaskow, "The Coming of Lilith: Toward a Feminist Theology," in *Womanspirit Rising: A Feminist Reader in*

Religion, ed. Carol P. Christ and Judith Plaskow (San Francisco: Harper & Row, 1979), p. 207.

3   Sandra Gilbert and Susan Gubar, *The Madwoman in the Attic: The Woman Writer and the Nineteenth-Century Literary Imagination* (New Haven: Yale University Press, 1979), p. 35.

4   Plaskow, "The Coming of Lilith," p. 206.

5   Mary Daly, *Beyond God the Father: Toward A Philosophy of Women's Liberation* (Boston: Beacon Press, 1973), p. 67.

6   Patricia Meyer Spacks, *The Female Imagination* (New York: Avon, 1976), p. 402.

7   Judith Fryer, *The Faces of Eve: Women in the Nineteenth-Century American Novel* (New York: Oxford University Press, 1976), pp. 256–57.

8   Spacks, *The Female Imagination*, p. 396.

9   Ibid., p. 398.

10 De Beauvoir, *The Second Sex*, p. 689.

BIBLIOGRAPHY

LITERATURE DISCUSSED

The following works are discussed or referred to in the text. Page citations in the text refer to the editions listed below.

Arnow, Harriette. *The Dollmaker*. New York: Avon, 1972.

Atwood, Margaret. *The Edible Woman*. New York: Popular Library, 1976.

———. *Lady Oracle*. New York: Avon, 1978.

———. *Life Before Man*. New York: Simon and Schuster, 1979.

———. *Surfacing*. New York: Popular Library, 1976.

Barfoot, Joan. *Abra*. New York: Signet, 1979.

Dillard, Annie. *Holy the Fin*. New York: Bantam, 1979.

———. *Pilgrim at Tinker Creek*. New York: Bantam, 1974.

Drabble, Margaret. *The Realms of Gold*. New York: Popular Library, 1977.

Gearhart, Sally Miller. *The Wanderground*. Watertown, Mass.: Persephone Press, 1978.

Gilman, Charlotte Perkins, *Herland*. New York: Pantheon, 1979. (Original serial publication, 1915.)

Gordon, Mary. *The Company of Women*. New York: Random House, 1981.

———. *Final Payments*. New York: Ballantine, 1978.

Laurence, Margaret. *The Diviners*. Toronto: McClelland and Stewart, 1974.

Lessing, Doris. *Canopus in Argos: Archives; The Marriages Between Zones Three, Four, and Five*. New York: Knopf, 1980.

———. *Canopus in Argos: Archives; The Serian Experi-*

ments; The Report by Ambian II of the Five. New York: Knopf, 1981.

———. *Canopus in Argos: Archives; Re: Colonized Planet 5, Shikasta; Personal, Psychological, Historical Documents Relating to Visit by Johor (George Sherban), Emissary (Grade 9), 87th of the Period of the Last Days*. New York: Knopf, 1979.

———. *The Four-Gated City*. New York: Bantam, 1970.

———. *The Golden Notebook*. New York: Bantam, 1973.

———. *A Man and Two Women*. New York: Popular Library, 1963.

———. *The Memoirs of a Survivor*. New York: Bantam, 1976.

———. *A Proper Marriage*. New York: New American Library, 1970.

Millett, Kate. *The Basement*. New York: Simon and Schuster, 1979.

Morrison, Toni. *The Bluest Eye*. Pocket Books, 1972.

———. *Song of Solomon*. New York: New American Library, 1978.

———. *Sula*. New York: Bantam, 1975.

Piercy, Marge. *Woman on the Edge of Time*. New York: Fawcett, 1976.

Russ, Joanna. *The Female Man*. New York: Bantam, 1975.

Wittig, Monique. *Les Guilleres*. Trans. David Le Vay. New York: Avon, 1973.

SECONDARY WORKS

Alder, Margot. *Drawing Down the Moon; Witches, Druids, Goddess-Worshippers and Other Pagans in America Today*. New York: Viking, 1979.

Atwood, Margaret. *Survival: A Thematic Guide to Canadian Literature*. Toronto: House of Anansi Press, 1972.

Auerbach, Nina. *Communities of Women: An Idea in Fiction*. Cambridge: Harvard University Press, 1978.

Bachofen, J. J. *Myth, Religion, and Mother Right.* Trans. Ralph Manheim. Princeton: Princeton University Press, 1954.

Beauvoir, Simone de. *The Second Sex.* Trans. H. M. Parshley. New York: Bantam, 1961.

Campbell, Joseph. *Hero with a Thousand Faces.* New York: Meridian, 1956.

———. *The Masks of God.* New York: Viking, 1969.

Chesler, Phyllis. *Women and Madness.* New York: Avon, 1972.

Christ, Carol P. *Diving Deep and Surfacing: Women Writers on Spiritual Quest.* Boston: Beacon Press, 1980.

———, and Judith Plaskow, eds. *Womanspirit Rising: A Feminist Reader in Religion.* San Francisco: Harper & Row, 1979.

Daly Mary. *Beyond God the Father: Toward a Philosophy of Women's Liberation.* Boston: Beacon Press, 1973.

———. *The Church and the Second Sex.* New York: Harper & Row, 1975.

———. *Gyn/Ecology: The Metaethics of Radical Feminism.* Boston: Beacon Press, 1978.

Davidson, Cathy N., and E. M. Broner, eds. *The Lost Tradition: Mothers and Daughters in Literature.* New York: Ungar, 1980.

Davis, Elizabeth Gould. *The First Sex.* New York: Putnam, 1971.

Diner, Helen. *Mothers and Amazons: The First Feminine History of Culture.* New York: Anchor/Doubleday, 1973.

Dinnerstein, Dorothy. *The Mermaid and the Minotaur: Sexual Arrangements and Human Malaise.* New York: Harper, 1976.

Firestone, Shulamith. *The Dialectic of Sex: The Case for a Feminist Revolution.* New York: Bantam, 1971.

Fremantle, Anne. *Woman's Way to God.* New York: St. Martin's Press, 1977.

Friedan, Betty. *The Feminine Mystique.* New York: Norton, 1970.

Frye, Northrop. *Secular Scripture: A Study of the Structure of Romance.* Cambridge: Harvard University Press, 1976.

Fryer, Judith. *The Faces of Eve: Women in the Nineteenth-Century American Novel*. New York: Oxford University Press, 1976.

Fuller, Margaret. *Woman in the Nineteenth Century*. New York, Norton, 1971.

Gibson, Graeme. *Eleven Canadian Novelists*. Toronto: House of Anansi Press, 1973.

Gilbert, Sandra, and Susan Gubar. *The Madwoman in the Attic: The Woman Writer and the Nineteenth-Century Imagination*. New Haven: Yale University Press, 1979.

Gilman, Charlotte Perkins. *His Religion and Hers: A Study of the Faith of Our Fathers and the Work of Our Mothers*. Westport: Hyperion Press, 1976 (reprint of 1923 edition).

Ginzberg, Louis. *The Legends of the Jews*. Philadelphia: The Jewish Publication Society of America, 1909.

Goldenberg, Naomi R. *The Changing of the Gods: Feminism and the End of Traditional Religion*. Boston: Beacon Press, 1979.

Graves, Robert. *The White Goddess: A Historical Grammar of Poetic Myth*. New York: Farrar, Straus and Giroux, 1966.

Griffin, Susan. *Woman and Nature: The Roaring inside Her*. New York: Harper & Row, 1978.

Harding, Esther. *Woman's Mysteries, Ancient and Modern*. New York: Bantam, 1973.

Hoch-Smith, Judith, and Anita Spring, eds. *Women in Ritual and Symbolic Roles*. New York: Plenum Press, 1978.

Jung, Carl G. *The Collected Works of Carl G. Jung*. Trans. R. F. C. Hull. New York: Pantheon, 1953.

Kolbenschlag, Madonna. *Kiss Sleeping Beauty Good-Bye: Breaking the Spell of Feminine Myths and Models*. New York: Doubleday, 1979.

Lane, Gary, ed. *Sylvia Plath: New Views on the Poetry*. Baltimore: Johns Hopkins University Press, 1979.

Lewis, R. W. B. *The American Adam: Innocence, Tragedy, and Tradition in the Nineteenth Century*. Chicago: University of Chicago Press, 1955.

Marx, Leo. *The Machine in the Garden: Technology and the*

Pastoral Ideal in America. New York: Oxford University Press, 1964.

Merchant, Carolyn. *The Death of Nature: Women, Ecology, and the Scientific Revolution.* San Francisco: Harper & Row, 1979.

Ochs, Carol. *Behind the Sex of God: Toward a New Consciousness Transcending Matriarchy and Patriarchy.* Boston: Beacon Press, 1977.

Pagels, Elaine. *The Gnostic Gospels.* New York: Random House, 1979.

Porterfield, Amanda. *Feminine Spirituality in America from Sarah Edwards to Martha Graham.* Philadelphia: Temple University Press, 1980.

Reik, Theodor. *The Creation of Woman: A Psychoanalytic Inquiry into the Myth of Eve.* New York: McGraw-Hill, 1973.

Reuther, Rosemary Radford. *New Woman, New Earth: Sexist Ideologies and Human Liberation.* New York: Seabury Press, 1975.

————, and Eleanor McLaughlin, eds. *Women of Spirit: Female Leadership in the Jewish and Christian Traditions.* New York: Simon and Schuster, 1979.

Rich, Adrienne. *Of Woman Born: Motherhood as Experience and Institution.* New York: Bantam, 1977.

Rigney, Barbara Hill. *Madness and Sexual Politics in the Feminist Novel: Studies in Bronte, Woolf, Lessing, and Atwood.* Madison: University of Wisconsin Press, 1978.

Rubenstein, Roberta. *The Novelistic Vision of Doris Lessing: Breaking the Forms of Consciousness.* Urbana: University of Illinois Press, 1979.

Spacks, Patricia Meyer. *The Female Imagination.* New York: Avon, 1976.

Stanton, Elizabeth Cady. *The Woman's Bible.* New York: Arno Press, 1974 (reprint of 1895 edition).

Starhawk. *The Spiral Dance: A Rebirth of the Ancient Religion of the Great Goddess.* San Francisco: Harper & Row, 1979.

Stone, Merlin, *When God Was a Woman.* New York: Dial Press, 1976.

Walker, Alice. "In Search of Our Mother's Gardens." In *Working It Out*. ed. Sara Ruddick and Pamela Daniels. New York: Pantheon, 1977.

Warner, Marina. *Alone of All Her Sex: The Myth and the Cult of the Virgin Mary*. New York: Pocket Books, 1976.

Weil, Simone. *Waiting for God*. Trans. Emma Crawford. New York: Harper & Row, 1973.

Ziolkowski, Theodore. *Fictional Transfigurations of Jesus*. Princeton: Princeton University Press, 1972.

INDEX

JACKET DESIGNED BY IRVING PERKINS ASSOCIATES
COMPOSED BY PIED TYPER, LINCOLN, NEBRASKA
MANUFACTURED BY CUSHING-MALLOY, INC.
ANN ARBOR, MICHIGAN
TEXT AND DISPLAY LINES ARE SET IN CALEDONIA

Library of Congress Cataloging in Publication Data
Rigney, Barbara Hill, 1938–
Lilith's daughters.
Bibliography: pp. 109–114.
Includes index.
1. American fiction—Women authors—History
and criticism   2. Women and religion in
literature.   3. Religion in literature.
4. Women in literature.   5. American fiction—
20th century—History and criticism.
6. English fiction—Women authors—History
and criticism.   7. English fiction—20th
century—History and criticism.   I. Title.
PS374.W6R5   813'.54'099287   81–70012
ISBN 0–299–08960–6   AACR2